Trick or Treat

The Shocking Truth Behind Halloween

TRICK OR TREAT: THE SHOCKING TRUTH BEHIND HALLOWEEN

First edition. October 15, 2024.

ISBN: 979-8227843012

Written by A.D. Wryte.

Table of Contents

Introduction: The Pumpkin-Spiced Truth

Picture this: It's Halloween night, 2019. I'm decked out in what I thought was the perfect costume - a life-sized, incredibly realistic hot dog. As I waddled down the street, basking in the admiration of fellow trick-or-treaters, disaster struck. A pack of neighborhood dogs, enticed by my meaty aroma, decided I was the world's largest chew toy. What followed was a chaotic chase scene that would put any slasher film to shame, ending with me trapped up a tree, my costume in tatters, and a newfound appreciation for the complexities of Halloween.

This, dear reader, is the essence of Halloween - a holiday that blends the ridiculous with the sublime, the scary with the sweet, and the ancient with the modern. It's a night when we willingly let our children dress as demons and beg for candy from strangers, a concept that would horrify us on any other day of the year. But how did we get here? Why do millions of people around the world eagerly anticipate a holiday that, at its core, is about confronting death and fear?

In this book, we're going to unwrap Halloween like a fun-sized Snickers bar, peeling back the layers to reveal the nutty, chewy, and sometimes unsavory center of this beloved holiday. We'll explore everything from its ancient Celtic roots to its modern-day multibillion-dollar industry status. Along the way, we'll encounter witch hunts (both literal and metaphorical), moral panics, environmental concerns, and enough sugar to send the entire population of Rhode Island into a diabetic coma.

But why, you might ask, should you trust me as your guide through this haunted history? Well, aside from my aforementioned expertise in outrunning canines while dressed as processed meat, I've spent years researching and experiencing Halloween in all its glory and gore. From the pumpkin patches of the Midwest to the vampire-themed nightclubs of Transylvania, I've seen it all. And now, I'm here to share these insights with you, served with a side of humor and a healthy dose of critical analysis.

So grab your candy bucket, don your costume, and prepare to see Halloween in a whole new light. By the time we're done, you'll never look at a jack-o'-lantern the same way again. And who knows? You might even learn why bobbing for apples is less a festive game and more a medieval version of Tinder.

Let's begin our journey into the heart of Halloween. Just remember - whatever you do, don't split up to investigate that strange noise. That never ends well.

Chapter 1: The Roots of All Evil (or Just Candy Corn?)

If you've ever bitten into a piece of candy corn and thought, "This tastes like the fossilized dreams of disappointed children," you're not alone. But before we judge this waxy, tri-colored abomination too harshly, let's take a moment to consider its ancestors – the ancient Celtic festival of Samhain.

Picture this: It's 2,000 years ago in what's now Ireland. The harvest is in, winter is coming (cue the Game of Thrones theme), and the ancient Celts are gearing up for their New Year's Eve bash on October 31st. But this isn't just any party. The Celts believed that on this night, the boundary between the world of the living and the dead became as thin as your cousin's "sexy ghost" costume.

Samhain (pronounced "sow-in," not "sam-hain" – save that mispronunciation for your next Halloween party to sound extra pretentious) was essentially the Celtic version of "The Purge," minus the government-sanctioned murder. The Celts would dress up in animal heads and skins, not to score candy, but to avoid being kidnapped by roaming ghosts. It's like Uber's surge pricing, but for souls.

Now, you might be thinking, "That's all well and good, but how did we get from animal carcass couture to Marvel superhero costumes and fun-sized Snickers?" Well, dear reader, blame it on the Romans. As they did with most things (roads, aqueducts, orgies), the Romans came, saw, and rebranded.

When they conquered Celtic lands in 43 A.D., they folded Samhain into their own fall festivals. There was Feralia, a day in late October to commemorate the dead (because nothing says "party" like remembering your deceased great-aunt Claudia), and Pomona, a day to honor the Roman goddess of fruit and trees. Incidentally, Pomona's symbol was the apple, which might explain why we still bob for apples at Halloween. Although, if you've ever stuck your face in a bucket of water surrounded by your peers, you'll agree it feels less like honoring a goddess and more like a soggy form of public humiliation.

Fast forward a few centuries, and the Christian church, in its infinite wisdom, decided that the best way to deal with these pagan holidays was to slap a "new and improved" label on them. In the 8th century, Pope Gregory III designated November 1 as a day to honor all saints. The evening before became known as All Hallows' Eve, which eventually got shortened to "Halloween," because even in the 8th century, people couldn't resist a good abbreviation.

But how did this Celtic-Roman-Christian mash-up cross the pond to America, land of supersized everything? For that, we can thank the Irish – not for the first or last time when it comes to holidays involving excessive drinking. The potato famine of the 1840s sent waves of Irish immigrants to America, and they brought their Halloween traditions with them. The Americans, always eager for a reason to party, took to Halloween like a witch to a broomstick.

At first, Halloween in America was a relatively tame affair – think harvest celebrations with a dash of matchmaking. Young women would try to divine the name of their future husbands by doing things like throwing apple peels over their shoulders. Spoiler alert: This method of finding true love is about as effective as swiping right on everyone on Tinder.

But as Halloween spread across the country, it began to evolve. By the 1920s and 1930s, Halloween had become a community-centered holiday with parades and town-wide parties. And then, sometime in the 1950s, someone had the brilliant idea to capitalize on this holiday by marketing cheap plastic masks and buckets of cavity-inducing sweets to children.

And just like that, the Halloween industrial complex was born. From the sacred Celtic festival to the sugar-fueled frenzy we know today, Halloween has undergone more transformations than a

Transformer on a sugar high. But at its core, it remains a night when the ordinary rules don't apply, when we confront our fears of death and the unknown – and then demand free candy as compensation.

So the next time you pop a piece of candy corn in your mouth (why would you do that to yourself?), remember: you're not just consuming a questionable confection. You're partaking in a tradition that's been evolving for over two millennia. Now that's a trick and a treat.

Now that we've established the Celtic-Roman-Christian cocktail that birthed Halloween, let's delve deeper into how this spooky celebration spread its tendrils across the globe. Because nothing says "cultural phenomenon" quite like convincing people worldwide to dress up as sexy versions of household appliances.

As we leap forward into medieval times, Halloween began to take on a distinctly Christian flavor, like a communion wafer dipped in pumpkin spice. The church, ever the master of rebranding, turned Samhain into "All Souls' Day" on November 2nd. This was a day when the living prayed for the souls of the dead, which, let's face it, is a much more somber affair than running around in a Pikachu onesie asking for candy.

But old habits die hard, and the pagan traditions refused to go quietly into the night. People continued to celebrate Halloween with bonfires, parades, and costumes. In a practice called "souling," poor people would go door-to-door on All Souls' Day, begging for food in exchange for prayers for the dead. It was like a medieval version of Postmates, but with more spiritual benefits and fewer delivery fees.

In Scotland and Ireland, young people took part in a tradition called "guising," dressing up in costumes and accepting food, wine, or money in exchange for songs, poems, or jokes. It was essentially an open mic night with better snacks. This tradition, of course, is the precursor to modern trick-or-treating, minus the threat of property damage if the performance wasn't up to par.

No discussion of Halloween's history would be complete without mentioning the Salem Witch Trials of 1692-1693. This wasn't so much a Halloween celebration as it was a cautionary tale about what happens when mass hysteria meets terrible judicial practices.

In colonial Massachusetts, over 200 people were accused of witchcraft, with 19 being executed by hanging. It was like a really dark episode of "Law & Order: Special Victims Unit," but with more bonnets and fewer Miranda rights. The trials serve as a stark reminder of the very real fears and superstitions that once surrounded witchcraft – fears that Halloween now commodifies in the form of green face paint and pointy hats.

Ironically, modern-day Salem has fully embraced its spooky history, becoming a major Halloween tourist destination. Nothing says "we've learned from our mistakes" quite like turning a site of historical injustice into a theme park where you can buy witch-themed shot glasses.

As we sashay into the Victorian era, Halloween took on a decidedly more romantic tone. Young people in America started using Halloween as an excuse for matchmaking parties, which were less about summoning spirits and more about scoping out potential mates.

These parties involved games like "snap-apple," where players tried to bite an apple suspended on a string – a game that seems designed solely to make people look ridiculous in front of their crushes. Another popular activity was to peel an apple in one long strip, then throw the peel over your shoulder. The shape it formed on the ground was supposed to reveal the first letter of your future spouse's name. It was basically the 19th-century equivalent of a BuzzFeed quiz, but with more potential for food waste.

As we mentioned earlier, the Irish potato famine of the 1840s led to a mass migration of Irish people to America. But the Halloween exchange wasn't just one-way. As Americans embraced and commercialized Halloween, these new traditions began to filter back to Europe.

By the early 20th century, Halloween parties were becoming popular in England. The British, never ones to pass up an opportunity for a good costume party, took to the holiday with gusto. Although, in true British fashion, they managed to make it slightly more refined. Instead of asking "Trick or treat?", British children would say "Penny for the Guy," collecting money for fireworks to celebrate Guy Fawkes Night on November 5th. Leave it to the British to combine Halloween with a celebration of a failed attempt to blow up Parliament.

Now, let's talk about the crown jewel of modern Halloween: trick-or-treating. This tradition as we know it today didn't really take off until the 1930s in America. It was a way to provide controlled mischief for kids during the Great Depression, because nothing lifts the spirits during economic hardship quite like free candy.

The phrase "trick or treat" first appeared in print in 1927, in an Alberta, Canada newspaper. The article described how "youthful tormentors" were visiting houses demanding either a "trick or treat." It's worth noting that back then, the "trick" part was taken more seriously. If treats weren't provided, pranksters might soap windows, overturn trash cans, or engage in other minor acts of vandalism. It was like a protection racket run by children hopped up on sugar.

The practice was interrupted briefly during World War II due to sugar rationing. Apparently, even the Axis powers couldn't stop Halloween, but limited access to sugar could. However, when the war ended and the sugar flowed freely again, trick-or-treating came back with a vengeance.

By the 1950s, trick-or-treating had become a full-blown phenomenon, aided in no small part by the media. The Peanuts gang went trick-or-treating in the comic strips, and popular TV shows like "The Adventures of Ozzie and Harriet" featured trick-or-treating episodes. It was as if the entire country collectively decided that what we really needed was an annual event where we encourage children to take candy from strangers.

As trick-or-treating took off, businesses were quick to capitalize on the trend. Candy companies, which had previously focused their marketing efforts on Christmas and Easter, realized they had a potential goldmine on their hands. They began producing smaller, individually wrapped candies specifically for trick-or-treaters.

The first Halloween-specific candy was Candy Corn, invented in the 1880s by George Renninger of the Wunderle Candy Company. Brach's Confections began mass-producing it in 1898, and it's been dividing Halloween enthusiasts ever since. Love it or hate it, you have to admire a candy that looks like it hasn't changed its recipe or design in over a century.

By the 1960s, companies like Mars and Hershey's were all in on the Halloween game, producing special Halloween-themed packaging for their candies. The Mars company introduced the "fun size" candy bar in 1961, which is arguably the least accurate name ever given to a product. There's nothing fun about getting less candy, Mars. Nothing.

As Halloween became more popular, the costume industry exploded. In the early days, most Halloween costumes were homemade affairs. People would dress up as ghosts, witches, or other traditional spooky characters using whatever they had on hand. It was a simpler time, when a sheet with eyeholes cut out was considered a perfectly acceptable costume.

But as the holiday grew, so did the demand for ready-made costumes. Companies like Ben Cooper, Inc. and Collegeville began mass-producing inexpensive costumes in the 1930s. Many of these early costumes were based on popular cartoon characters or public figures. Imagine a time when you could buy a mask of the current President for Halloween. On second thought, maybe some things are better left in the past.

By the 1970s and 1980s, Halloween costumes had become big business. Movie characters, pop culture icons, and even household products became popular costume choices. It was during this time that we saw the rise of the "sexy" costume trend, proving that any concept, no matter how mundane or terrifying, can be made "sexy" with the addition of fishnet stockings and a miniskirt. Sexy potato? Check. Sexy Pennywise the Clown? Unfortunately, also check.

As American pop culture spread around the world in the latter half of the 20th century, so too did Halloween. Countries that had never celebrated the holiday began to adopt it, often blending it with their own traditions.

In Japan, for instance, Halloween has become incredibly popular in recent years, particularly in urban areas. However, trick-or-treating hasn't caught on. Instead, Halloween in Japan is more about cosplay and parties. Leave it to Japan to take costume-wearing to the next level.

In Mexico, Halloween coincides with the traditional Día de los Muertos (Day of the Dead) celebrations. While these are separate holidays with different origins, they've begun to blend in some areas, creating a unique cultural fusion. It's like a holiday version of Tex-Mex cuisine, but with more skulls and fewer burritos.

Even in parts of Europe where Halloween wasn't traditionally celebrated, the American version of the holiday has gained a foothold. Although, in true European fashion, they've managed to make it seem slightly more sophisticated. In France, for example, Halloween parties might involve wine tastings rather than bobbing for apples. Because nothing says "spooky" quite like a good Bordeaux.

As we've entered the 21st century, Halloween has continued to evolve. Social media has transformed the way we celebrate the holiday. Instagram and Pinterest are flooded with costume ideas and elaborate Halloween decorations, setting unrealistic expectations for the rest of us who can barely manage to carve a simple jack-o'-lantern without requiring stitches.

Halloween has also become a major event in the online gaming world. Many popular video games offer special Halloween-themed events or skins, allowing players to bring the spooky spirit into their virtual worlds. It's a time when even the most hardened first-person shooter players might find themselves hunting for virtual pumpkins instead of enemy combatants.

Virtual and augmented reality technologies are also changing the face of Halloween. Haunted house experiences can now be had from the comfort of your own home, although the effect is somewhat diminished when you can simply take off the headset to escape the monsters.

As we look to the future, it's clear that Halloween will continue to evolve. Climate change concerns are leading to more environmentally-friendly celebration options, from biodegradable decorations to plant-based candies. The rise of food allergies and dietary restrictions is changing the treat landscape, with the Teal Pumpkin Project encouraging non-food treats for trick-or-treaters.

But at its core, Halloween remains a time when we confront our fears, indulge our fantasies, and consume far more sugar than any medical professional would recommend. It's a holiday that has survived centuries of cultural changes, religious opposition, and the invention of candy corn. If that's not proof of Halloween's staying power, I don't know what is.

So the next time you find yourself wondering why you're dressed as a giant avocado, demanding candy from your neighbors, remember: you're participating in a tradition that stretches back over two millennia. And really, is there any better way to honor our ancestors than by gorging ourselves on fun-sized candy bars while watching "Hocus Pocus" for the hundredth time? I think not.

Chapter 2: Costume Drama
A Fashionable History of Halloween Attire

If you've ever found yourself standing in front of a mirror on October 31st, questioning your life choices while dressed as a "sexy avocado toast," you're participating in a tradition as old as Halloween itself. Well, maybe not the "sexy avocado toast" part – our ancestors had slightly more dignity. But the act of donning a costume for Halloween is a practice that's been around for centuries, evolving from a way to ward off evil spirits to a multi-billion dollar industry that turns even the most mundane objects into potential outfits.

Let's rewind to where it all began, shall we? The ancient Celts, those plucky ancestors of modern-day Irish, Scottish, and Welsh people, didn't dress up to get Instagram likes or win costume contests. No, their reasons were far more practical: they were trying not to get kidnapped by ghosts.

During Samhain, the Celts believed that the veil between the world of the living and the dead was at its thinnest. This meant that spirits could cross over, which was about as welcome as your neighbor's off-key karaoke at 2 AM. To avoid being recognized by these wandering spirits, people would disguise themselves.

But we're not talking about dropping by the local Party City for a pre-packaged costume. These early costumes were serious business, often involving animal heads and skins. Imagine a whole village dressed like extras from a low-budget production of "The Lion King," and you're on the right track.

These costumes served a dual purpose. Not only did they hide you from spirits, but they also allowed you to imitate and honor the dead. It was like a prehistoric version of cosplay, but with 100% more actual animal parts and 100% less body glitter.

As we move into the Middle Ages, the practice of dressing up took on new dimensions. With the spread of Christianity, Samhain morphed into All Souls' Day, but the costume tradition persisted. People would dress as angels, saints, and devils – a sort of "Heaven and Hell" theme party, if you will.

In Scotland and Ireland, young people took part in a tradition called "guising." They would dress in costume and go door-to-door performing songs, poems, or jokes in exchange for food or money. It was like an open mic night, but with better snacks and a more forgiving audience. These guisers often wore masks, which were believed to ward off evil spirits. Because nothing says "begone, foul demon" quite like a poorly constructed papier-mâché mask.

The costumes of this era were a far cry from the mass-produced outfits we see today. Most were homemade, using whatever materials were on hand. A sheet with eyeholes? Congratulations, you're a ghost. A pointy hat and a broom? Witch, please. It was a simpler time, when creativity and a lack of options went hand in hand.

As we sashay into the Victorian era, Halloween costumes took on a decidedly more elaborate – and sometimes bizarre – tone. The Victorians, never ones to do things by halves, embraced the concept of the Halloween masquerade party with gusto.

These weren't your average costume parties. Oh no. The Victorians took it to a whole new level of weird. Popular costumes included "Locomotive" (yes, as in the train), "Hornet's Nest" (complete with paper wasps), and "Electric Light" (which involved wearing a wire helmet with a light bulb attached). It was as if they were playing a game of "how can we make this as uncomfortable and impractical as possible?"

But it wasn't all bizarre contraptions and questionable choices. The Victorian era also saw the rise of more recognizable Halloween staples. Witch costumes became popular, although they were often more glamorous than scary. The image of the witch had begun its long journey from terrifying hag to "I got this at Hot Topic."

Ghost costumes also evolved during this time. No longer content with a simple sheet, Victorian ghosts often wore elaborate white gowns adorned with fake blood or chains. It was like "Ghostbusters" meets "Project Runway."

As Halloween made its way to America, so did the tradition of dressing up. Initially, costumes in the New World were similar to their European counterparts – lots of ghosts, witches, and devils. But as with many things, Americans soon put their own spin on it.

The late 19th and early 20th centuries saw the rise of Halloween parties as social events, particularly for young adults. Costumes at these parties often reflected the pop culture of the time. Silent film stars, flappers, and historical figures were all popular choices. It was a time when you could show up to a party dressed as Teddy Roosevelt and not have people assume you were making some kind of political statement.

But it wasn't all glamour and pop culture references. Rural America had its own Halloween costume traditions, often involving pranks and mischief. Young men would often dress in drag, not as a statement of gender expression, but as a way to confuse and surprise their neighbors while engaging in Halloween hijinks. It was a simpler time, when a man in a dress was considered the height of comedic genius.

The real turning point for Halloween costumes came in the 1930s, with the rise of mass-produced costumes. Companies like Ben Cooper, Inc. and Collegeville began churning out affordable, ready-made costumes, often based on popular characters from comics, movies, and TV shows.

These early mass-produced costumes were... let's say, an acquired taste. They typically consisted of a plastic mask and a printed fabric smock. The masks were often terrifying, but not in the way they were intended to be. Many a child of the 1960s and 70s still wakes up in a cold sweat, haunted by memories of trying to breathe through tiny nose holes while peering through misaligned eye slots.

But despite their shortcomings, these costumes were a hit. For the first time, kids could easily transform into their favorite characters. Want to be Batman? No need to spend weeks crafting a utility belt out of egg cartons. Just slap on a mask and a smock with "BATMAN" helpfully printed across the chest (in case anyone was confused by the bat ears and cape), and you're good to go.

As we moved into the latter half of the 20th century, Halloween costumes became increasingly tied to pop culture. Every blockbuster movie, hit TV show, or popular musician became fodder for costume ideas.

The 1970s and 80s saw a parade of Luke Skywalkers, Princess Leias, Michael Jacksons, and Madonna wannabes hitting the streets every Halloween. It was a time when your costume choice said a lot about your pop culture allegiances. Showing up as a Trekkie to a party full of Star Wars fans? May the Force be with you, because you're going to need it.

This trend has only intensified in recent years. In the age of social media, Halloween has become a way to showcase your cultural savvy. Dressing as a character from the latest Netflix sensation or a meme that went viral last week? You're not just wearing a costume; you're making a statement about your finger-on-the-pulse coolness.

No discussion of modern Halloween costumes would be complete without addressing the elephant in the room – or should I say, the scantily clad elephant in the room. I'm talking, of course, about the phenomenon of "sexy" costumes.

It's hard to pinpoint exactly when this trend started, but by the early 2000s, it was in full swing. Suddenly, any concept, no matter how decidedly un-sexy, could be made "sexy" with the addition of fishnet stockings and a miniskirt. Sexy nurse? Amateur hour. Sexy pizza? Now we're talking. Sexy Mr. Rogers? ... Let's not.

This trend has been both embraced and criticized. On one hand, it's been seen as a way for people (particularly women) to express their sexuality in a safe, fun environment. On the other hand, it's been criticized for promoting unrealistic body standards and turning every costume into a potential Victoria's Secret runway show.

But love them or hate them, sexy costumes have become a Halloween staple. They've even spawned their own sub-genre of humor, with people creating increasingly ridiculous "sexy" versions of decidedly un-sexy things. Sexy hand sanitizer, anyone? (Yes, that was a real costume in 2020. Because nothing says "alluring" quite like alcohol-based gels.)

In recent years, there's been a resurgence of interest in DIY costumes. Thanks in part to social media platforms like Pinterest and Instagram, homemade costumes have made a comeback. But these aren't your grandma's sheet ghost costumes. Oh no.

Modern DIY costumes range from clever wordplay (like dressing as a "ceiling fan" complete with team jerseys and a foam finger) to incredibly elaborate recreations of movie scenes or works of art. It's as if the entire Halloween-celebrating world collectively decided to put the costume industry on notice: "Anything you can do, we can do better... and probably cheaper."

This trend has led to some truly impressive displays of creativity. People have transformed themselves into everything from lifelike animals to walking optical illusions. It's gotten to the point where simply buying a costume off the rack almost feels like cheating.

Of course, for every stunning homemade costume that makes the rounds on social media, there are countless DIY disasters. We've all seen those "nailed it" memes comparing the Pinterest ideal to the sad reality. But hey, at least those folks get points for trying, right?

As our society has become more culturally aware, so too has our approach to Halloween costumes. Costumes that might have been considered acceptable (or even funny) in the past are now rightly recognized as offensive and problematic.

Cultural appropriation has become a major topic of discussion around Halloween. Costumes that reduce entire cultures to stereotypical elements have faced increasing criticism. The days of people thoughtlessly donning sombreros and fake mustaches or wearing blackface are (thankfully) coming to an end.

This has led to some much-needed conversations about respect, representation, and the impact of our costume choices. It's also led to some truly spectacular displays of missing the point, with people complaining that they can't dress as whatever they want anymore. To which the rest of us say: read the room, Karen.

But it's not just cultural insensitivity that's come under fire. In recent years, there's been pushback against costumes that make light of serious issues or tragedies. Dressing as a "sexy ebola nurse" or a victim of a recent natural disaster? Maybe reconsider your life choices.

So where do we go from here? As we look to the future, it's clear that Halloween costumes will continue to evolve. Technology is already playing a bigger role, with costumes incorporating LED lights, sound effects, and even augmented reality elements.

We're also seeing a trend towards more inclusive Halloween celebrations, with costume companies offering a wider range of sizes and adaptive costumes for people with disabilities. Because everyone deserves the chance to transform into someone (or something) else for a night.

Environmental concerns are also shaping the future of Halloween costumes. As awareness of the environmental impact of fast fashion grows, there's increasing interest in sustainable, reusable, or recyclable costume options. The days of cheap, wear-once polyester costumes may be numbered.

Virtual Halloween celebrations, which gained popularity during the COVID-19 pandemic, may also influence future costume trends.

When your Halloween party is on Zoom, does it matter if you're wearing pants with that elaborate top half of your costume? (The answer is yes, by the way. Always wear pants. You never know when you might have to stand up unexpectedly.)

As we've seen, Halloween costumes have come a long way from their origins as spirit-deceiving disguises. They've been shaped by cultural shifts, technological advancements, and changing social norms. They've been mass-produced, handmade, praised, criticized, and everything in between.

But at their core, Halloween costumes still serve the same basic function they always have: they allow us to step outside ourselves for a night. Whether we're dressing as our favorite movie character, a pun come to life, or yes, even a sexy avocado toast, costumes give us the freedom to be someone (or something) else for a while.

So this Halloween, as you're putting the finishing touches on your costume (or panic-buying something at the last minute because you forgot Halloween was coming up... again), take a moment to appreciate the rich history behind your disguise. Whether you're wearing a plastic mask with "SUPERHERO" stamped across the forehead or an intricately crafted recreation of Marie Antoinette's entire wardrobe, you're participating in a tradition that stretches back centuries.

And who knows? Maybe in another hundred years, people will look back at our costume choices with the same mixture of amusement and bafflement that we view Victorian "Electric Light" costumes. But that's the beauty of Halloween – it's always evolving, always reflecting our current culture, and always giving us an excuse to wear ridiculous outfits in public.

So go forth and costume, my friends. Just maybe leave the "sexy hand sanitizer" idea for another year. Some things are better left in 2020.

Chapter 3: Sweet Tooth for Profit
The Candy Industrial Complex

Ah, Halloween candy. That sugary siren call that turns even the most health-conscious among us into ravenous sugar fiends for one glorious night a year. But how did we get here? How did a holiday rooted in ancient Celtic traditions become synonymous with fun-sized candy bars and heated debates over the merits of candy corn? Buckle up, buttercup, because we're about to take a tour through the sticky, sweet history of Halloween candy.

Before we dive into the cavity-inducing world of modern Halloween candy, let's take a moment to appreciate what came before. In the early days of trick-or-treating, the "treats" were a far cry from the colorful, wrapper-crinkling delights we know today.

Back in the 1930s and 1940s, when trick-or-treating was first gaining popularity in the United States, children might receive apples, nuts, coins, or even small toys. Some particularly ambitious homeowners would hand out homemade treats like popcorn balls or cookies. It was a simpler time, when the phrase "razor blade in the apple" was just a twinkle in an urban legend writer's eye.

But let's be honest, if you handed out apples to trick-or-treaters today, you'd probably wake up to find your house covered in toilet paper. And not the good kind – we're talking single-ply, sandpaper-esque toilet paper. The kind that makes you question your life choices as you're scrubbing it off your prized azaleas.

So how did we transition from apples and nuts to the candy-coated extravaganza we know today? For that, we can thank (or blame, depending on your dentist's opinion) the major candy companies of the mid-20th century.

Companies like Hershey's, Mars, and Nestle saw an opportunity in Halloween that was sweeter than a block of pure sugar. Here was a holiday that practically begged for mass-produced, individually wrapped treats. It was like Christmas for candy companies, except instead of one jolly old elf distributing the goods, you had an entire nation of sugar-crazed children demanding treats with the threat of tricks looming over their neighbors' heads.

The candy companies launched aggressive marketing campaigns, positioning their products as the perfect Halloween treats. They introduced smaller, individually wrapped versions of their popular candies, dubbed "fun size" – a name that has been puzzling children for generations. After all, what's fun about getting less candy?

By the 1970s, these marketing efforts had paid off in a big way. Store-bought candy had become the standard for trick-or-treating, relegating homemade treats and fruit to the status of "disappointment" in the eyes of sugar-seeking children everywhere.

No discussion of Halloween candy would be complete without addressing the tricolored elephant in the room: candy corn. This waxy, triangular treat has been dividing Halloween enthusiasts since its invention in the 1880s.

Created by George Renninger of the Wunderle Candy Company, candy corn was originally called "Chicken Feed." It was marketed to rural America with the less-than-appetizing slogan, "Something worth crowing for." Because nothing says "delicious candy" quite like comparing it to what you feed your livestock.

Despite its questionable origins, candy corn quickly became associated with Halloween. Its orange, yellow, and white colors mirrored the colors of autumn, and its shape vaguely resembled a kernel of corn (if you squint really hard and maybe have had a few Halloween cocktails).

Today, candy corn remains a polarizing Halloween staple. Some people love it, some people hate it, and some people only eat it because it's there and they've already gone through all the "good" candy. It's the participation trophy of the candy world – nobody really wants it, but we keep producing it out of some misguided sense of tradition.

The 1980s brought a new challenge to the world of Halloween candy: paranoia. Urban legends about razor blades in apples and poisoned candy spread like wildfire, leading to a nationwide panic. Parents were encouraged to inspect their children's candy, hospitals offered to X-ray treat bags, and the phrase "stranger danger" entered the Halloween lexicon.

The irony? There has never been a confirmed case of a child being poisoned by Halloween candy from a stranger. The closest incident was a tragic case in 1974 when a father poisoned his own son's candy to collect on a life insurance policy. Which, let's be clear, is horrifying, but not quite the random-stranger-danger scenario that captured the public imagination.

Nevertheless, the candy scare had lasting effects on Halloween. It accelerated the shift towards commercially produced, individually wrapped candies. After all, if it comes in a sealed wrapper from a big-name company, it must be safe... right?

This panic also gave rise to alternative Halloween celebrations like "trunk-or-treat" events in church parking lots, where children collect candy from the trunks of cars belonging to people their parents know and trust. Because nothing says "spooky Halloween fun" quite like a church parking lot filled with suburban minivans.

By the 21st century, Halloween candy had become big business. Really big business. We're talking billions of dollars big. According to the National Retail Federation, Americans were expected to spend $3.1 billion on Halloween candy in 2022. That's a lot of fun-sized Snickers, folks.

This candy bonanza has led to some truly impressive (or terrifying, depending on your perspective) statistics. The average American consumes about 3.4 pounds of candy over the Halloween season. Given that the recommended daily sugar intake for an adult is about 30 grams (roughly 0.06 pounds), we're essentially eating about a month's worth of sugar in the span of a few days. Our pancreases must love us.

But it's not just about the volume of candy consumed. Halloween has become a battleground for candy companies, each vying to be the most coveted treat in the trick-or-treat bag. This has led to some truly spectacular marketing campaigns and limited-edition offerings.

Take, for example, the great M&M's color debate of 1995. Mars, the maker of M&M's, launched a nationwide vote to choose a new color to add to the mix. The contenders? Blue, pink, or purple. Blue won, in case you were wondering, beating out purple by a mere 54% to 41%. Pink trailed far behind at 5%, presumably because it was already spoken for by Strawberry Starburst.

This kind of marketing genius doesn't stop at color choices. We've seen glow-in-the-dark wrappers, "spooky" flavor combinations (blood orange chocolate, anyone?), and enough pumpkin spice variations to make a Starbucks barista blush.

But it's not all fun and games in the world of Halloween candy. The massive demand for cheap sweets has a darker side, particularly when it comes to the sourcing of key ingredients like cocoa.

Much of the world's cocoa is produced in West Africa, often under conditions that are far from sweet. Child labor and even forced labor have been persistent issues in the cocoa industry. It's a bitter pill to swallow when you realize that the chocolate bar you're munching on may have been produced under ethically questionable circumstances.

This realization has led to increased pressure on candy companies to ensure their supply chains are ethical and sustainable. Many major companies have made commitments to source only ethically produced cocoa, although progress has been slower than many would like.

It's a complex issue without easy solutions, but it's one that consumers are becoming increasingly aware of. So the next time you're choosing your Halloween candy, you might want to consider not just the flavor, but also the ethics behind the wrapper.

As if ethical concerns weren't enough to make you think twice about your candy consumption, there's also the small matter of, you know, health. In an era of increasing awareness about the dangers of excessive sugar consumption, Halloween candy has come under scrutiny.

The American Heart Association recommends that men consume no more than 36 grams of added sugar per day, and women no more than 25 grams. Now, consider that a single fun-sized Snickers bar contains about 8.5 grams of sugar. Do the math, and you'll realize that it doesn't take many of those "fun-sized" treats to blow past your daily sugar allowance.

This has led to a push for healthier Halloween alternatives. Some households have started giving out non-food treats like stickers or small toys. Others opt for "healthier" candy options, although the phrase "healthy candy" feels a bit like an oxymoron. It's like saying "delicious rice cake" or "exciting tax audit."

The Teal Pumpkin Project, started in 2012, aims to make Halloween more inclusive for children with food allergies by encouraging people to offer non-food treats. Participants place a teal-colored pumpkin outside their homes to signal that they have allergy-friendly options available. It's a heartwarming initiative, although one can't help but wonder if some kids are disappointed to receive a plastic spider ring instead of a Reese's Peanut Butter Cup.

One of the most contentious aspects of Halloween candy is the unofficial but fiercely debated candy hierarchy. Every child knows that not all Halloween candy is created equal. There are the coveted A-listers – your full-sized candy bars, your Reese's Cups, your Twix bars. Then there are the B-list candies – respectable, but not exciting. Your Skittles, your Starbursts, your M&M's.

And then... then there's the bottom tier. The candies that linger in the bottom of the bag long after Halloween has passed. We're talking

Bit-O-Honey, those weird peanut butter taffy things in the orange and black wrappers, and of course, the ever-divisive candy corn.

This hierarchy has real-world implications. It affects everything from trick-or-treating strategies (hit up the rich neighborhood first – they're more likely to have full-sized bars) to post-Halloween candy trading. Many a playground deal has been struck over a coveted King-Size Snickers or an unwanted box of Milk Duds.

In recent years, this unofficial hierarchy has even been given a pseudo-scientific treatment. Since 2006, candy enthusiasts David Ng and Ben Cohen have been conducting an annual online survey to determine the ultimate Halloween candy ranking. They call it the "Candy Hierarchy" and present their findings in a delightfully nerdy infographic each year.

Their findings confirm what many of us have long suspected: chocolate reigns supreme. Reese's Peanut Butter Cups, Twix, and Kit Kat consistently top the charts. At the bottom? Those aforementioned peanut butter taffies, along with Necco Wafers and, yes, candy corn.

As we look to the future, it's clear that Halloween candy will continue to evolve. We're already seeing trends towards more health-conscious options, sustainable packaging, and allergen-free alternatives. But don't worry – good old-fashioned sugar bombs aren't going anywhere anytime soon.

One interesting development is the rise of "craft" candy. Much like the craft beer movement, small-batch candy makers are creating unique, high-quality confections that put a gourmet spin on Halloween treats. Artisanal candy corn, anyone? (No, really, someone's probably making that somewhere.)

We're also seeing candy companies experiment with new flavors and combinations. Japanese Kit Kat, with its myriad of unusual flavors like wasabi and sake, has shown that consumers are willing to try some pretty out-there candy concepts. It's only a matter of time before we see these kinds of innovations hit the Halloween market. Sushi-flavored Skittles, perhaps?

Technology is also playing a role in shaping the future of Halloween candy. We've already seen candies with QR codes that link to augmented reality experiences. Imagine a future where your candy wrapper comes to life with spooky holograms, or where you can take a virtual tour of a candy factory just by scanning your chocolate bar.

But perhaps the most significant change we'll see in the future of Halloween candy is a shift towards more ethical and sustainable practices. As consumers become more conscious of the social and environmental impacts of their purchasing decisions, candy companies will need to adapt. We may see a future where all Halloween candy is fair trade, organic, and comes in biodegradable wrappers. Your great-grandchildren might be shocked to learn that we once handed out candy made with non-ethical chocolate wrapped in single-use plastics. The horror!

As we wrap up our tour through the sticky, sweet world of Halloween candy, it's clear that these tiny treats carry a lot of weight. They're not just sugar and food coloring – they're the stuff of childhood memories, cultural traditions, and heated debates.

Halloween candy has come a long way from its humble beginnings. It's weathered health scares, navigated changing consumer preferences, and somehow managed to keep candy corn in production despite its perpetual position at the bottom of every "favorite Halloween candy" list.

But at its core, Halloween candy is about more than just satisfying a sweet tooth. It's about the thrill of dumping out your trick-or-treat bag at the end of the night, sorting through your haul like a sugar-crazed dragon with its hoard. It's about the negotiations with siblings over who gets the last Twix bar. It's about the annual debate over whether candy corn is delicious or disgusting (it's disgusting, by the way, but you do you).

So this Halloween, as you're sneaking another fun-sized Snickers from your kid's trick-or-treat bag (don't worry, we won't tell), take a moment to appreciate the complex world behind that tiny treat. It's a world of innovation and tradition, of ethical dilemmas and sugar rushes, of childhood joy and adult nostalgia.

And remember – calories don't count on Halloween. At least, that's what we tell ourselves as we unwrap our fifth Reese's Cup of the night. Happy haunting, and may your Halloween be filled with all your favorite treats... even if that includes candy corn.

Chapter 4: Haunted Houses From Creaky Floorboards to Billion-Dollar Industry

Moving on to a slightly different topic. Picture this: You're walking through a dimly lit corridor, your heart pounding in your chest. Suddenly, a chainsaw-wielding maniac jumps out at you, and you scream so loud you're pretty sure you've woken up the actual dead. Congratulations! You've just experienced the joy (and terror) of a modern haunted house attraction. But how did we get here? How did we go from telling spooky stories around a campfire to paying good money to have the bejeezus scared out of us by actors in zombie makeup? Let's take a spine-tingling tour through the history and psychology of haunted attractions.

Humans have been scaring themselves for fun pretty much since we figured out that saber-toothed tigers weren't actually hiding behind every bush. The ancient Greeks and Romans had their myths of the underworld, medieval Europeans had their ghost stories, and Victorian-era folks had their séances and spirit photography. It seems we've always had a bit of a masochistic streak when it comes to fear.

But the modern haunted attraction as we know it has its roots in the 19th and early 20th centuries. In 1802, Marie Tussaud scandalized London society with her "Chamber of Horrors," a wax museum featuring the severed heads of executed French Revolution figures. It was gruesome, it was shocking, and people absolutely loved it. Because nothing says "fun day out" quite like staring at disturbingly realistic wax recreations of decapitated aristocrats.

The Grand Guignol theater in Paris, which operated from 1897 to 1962, took things a step further. Known for its naturalistic horror shows featuring graphic depictions of murder, torture, and madness, the Grand Guignol was essentially the slasher film of its day. Audience members would regularly faint during performances, which was seen as a mark of a particularly successful show. Talk about a tough crowd.

As we moved into the 20th century, haunted attractions began to take on a more recognizable form. Fairgrounds and carnivals started featuring "dark rides" and "ghost trains" – spooky attractions that would take riders through scenes of horror and supernatural terror. These rides were the precursors to the haunted houses we know today.

One of the earliest recorded haunted house attractions in the United States was the Orton and Spooner Ghost House, which opened in 1915 at the Hollycombe Steam Collection in England. It featured such cutting-edge scares as... things jumping out at you. Hey, it was 1915 – people were easily impressed back then.

In 1969, Disney upped the ante with the opening of the Haunted Mansion at Disneyland. This attraction combined state-of-the-art special effects with classic ghost story elements to create an experience that was spooky but family-friendly. It was haunted house meets theme park attraction, and it set a new standard for what a haunted attraction could be.

The Haunted Mansion was so popular that it spawned versions at other Disney parks around the world. It also inspired a truly terrible movie starring Eddie Murphy, but we don't talk about that. Some things are too horrifying even for a haunted attraction.

The 1970s and 1980s saw an explosion in the popularity of haunted attractions. This was due in part to the rise of slasher films and horror movies, which had primed audiences for more intense scares. It was also a result of advancements in special effects technology, which allowed haunted house designers to create more realistic and terrifying experiences.

One of the pioneers of the modern haunted attraction was the Knott's Scary Farm event at Knott's Berry Farm in California. Started in 1973, this annual Halloween event transformed the entire theme park into a giant haunted attraction. It featured multiple haunted mazes, scare zones, and roaming monsters. The event was a massive success and is still going strong today, inspiring similar events at theme parks around the world.

Another milestone in haunted attraction history was the opening of the Haunted Graveyard at Lake Compounce in Connecticut in 1991. This attraction covered over a mile of theme park space and took visitors on a 45-minute journey through various themed areas. It was one of the first haunted attractions to focus on creating a cohesive narrative experience rather than just a series of random scares.

Now, you might be wondering: why on earth do we willingly subject ourselves to these terrifying experiences? Why do we pay good money to have people in masks jump out at us and make us scream like startled goats? Well, it turns out there's some pretty interesting psychology behind our love of recreational terror.

According to psychologists, there are a few reasons why we enjoy being scared in controlled environments like haunted houses.

First up, we've got the adrenaline rush. Fear triggers the release of adrenaline and other chemicals in our bodies, creating a natural high. It's the same reason some people enjoy extreme sports or roller coasters. Essentially, haunted houses are like nature's drug dealers, but instead of selling you illicit substances, they're peddling good old-fashioned terror.

Then there's the sense of achievement. Surviving a scary experience, even a simulated one, can give us a sense of accomplishment and boost our confidence. It's like completing a marathon, but instead of running 26.2 miles, you're running from a guy in a hockey mask with a chainsaw. Same difference, really.

Interestingly, shared fear can also bring people closer together. That's why haunted houses are popular date activities. Nothing says romance like clinging to each other in abject terror, right? Although maybe save it for the third or fourth date, unless you want to see how your potential partner reacts under extreme stress on the first night out.

"Oh, you scream like a banshee and have a tendency to use others as human shields? Good to know."

Haunted houses also allow us to confront fears and explore dark themes in a safe, controlled environment. It's like dipping your toe into the pool of your deepest anxieties, but with the comfort of knowing you can get out whenever you want. And let's be honest, it's probably cheaper than therapy.

Finally, for some people, experiencing simulated fear can help them process and release real-life anxieties. It's a form of catharsis. Because sometimes, the best way to deal with the terrifying state of the world is to spend an evening being chased by zombies. It really puts things in perspective.

So there you have it, folks. The next time someone questions why you're willingly paying money to be terrified, you can confidently tell them it's not just for fun - it's for your psychological well-being. It's practically healthcare, really. Maybe we should be pushing for haunted house visits to be covered by insurance. Now that would be truly scary.

Of course, there's also the simple fact that some people just enjoy being scared. These are probably the same people who eat ghost peppers for fun and think skydiving sounds like a relaxing weekend activity.

Fast forward to today, and the haunted attraction industry has become a veritable horror show of success. According to the Haunted Attraction Association (yes, that's a real thing), there are over 1,200 professional haunted attractions in the United States alone, not counting the thousands of charity and amateur events that pop up every Halloween season.

The industry generates over $300 million in ticket sales annually, and that's not even counting associated spending on things like costumes, makeup, and therapy sessions for people who got a little too scared. When you factor in large-scale events like Universal Studios' Halloween Horror Nights, which can draw over 600,000 visitors in a single season, the economic impact of the haunted attraction industry is truly staggering.

But it's not just about the money. Modern haunted attractions have evolved into complex, highly produced experiences that blur the lines between theater, theme park, and interactive art installation.

Now, let's look at some trends shaping this industry of industrialized terror. First up, we've got immersive storytelling. Many high-end haunted attractions now feature complex narratives that unfold as visitors move through the experience. You're not just walking through a spooky house anymore; you're uncovering the dark secrets of a cursed family or escaping from a zombie apocalypse. It's like Shakespeare, if Shakespeare had written "Macbeth" with more chainsaws and fewer soliloquies.

Then there's interactive elements, where some attractions allow you to make choices that affect the outcome. It's like a choose-your-own-adventure book, but with more zombies and fewer opportunities to cheat by peeking at other pages. Will you take the creepy door on the left or the ominous trapdoor on the right? Either way, you're probably going to scream.

But wait, there's more! We've got virtual and augmented reality being incorporated into these houses of horror. Because apparently, regular reality isn't scary enough. Now you can experience the joy of being chased by a digital monster that only you can see. It's a great way to convince your friends that you're either incredibly brave or having a psychotic break.

And for those of you who find traditional haunted houses too tame, there's a growing sub-genre of "extreme" haunts that push the boundaries of what's considered acceptable. These often involve physical contact, isolation, and psychological manipulation. Nothing says "fun night out" quite like signing away your right to sue if you're traumatized, right? It's like a spa day, if spas were run by sadistic carnival workers.

But creating a successful haunted attraction is no easy feat. It requires a unique blend of artistic vision, psychological understanding, and technical know-how. Designers carefully control the pacing, alternating between moments of tension, release, and outright terror. It's like composing a symphony, but with more fake blood and animatronic monsters.

They also use misdirection, just like magicians. They might use a loud noise or bright light to draw your attention in one direction, only to have a scare come from somewhere completely unexpected. It's like a magic show, except instead of pulling a rabbit out of a hat, they're pulling the rug out from under your sense of security.

Sensory manipulation is another key tool in their arsenal of terror. They might use temperature changes, unpleasant smells, or disorienting lighting effects. Some attractions even use subtle low-frequency sound waves to create a sense of unease. It's all very scientific, in a mad scientist sort of way. They're basically using physics to make you pee your pants.

And let's not forget about the actors. The performers in a haunted attraction are crucial to its success. They undergo extensive training to learn how to scare effectively and safely. It's probably the only job where "made a grown man cry" is considered a positive performance review. Imagine that on your LinkedIn profile.

But like any industry, the world of haunted attractions has its share of controversies and challenges. There are safety concerns, with instances of injuries and even deaths at some attractions. Because nothing ruins a good scare quite like actual bodily harm.

There are also concerns about the psychological impact, especially on children or individuals with anxiety disorders. Some critics argue that extreme haunts, in particular, may be crossing ethical lines. It's a fine line between a fun fright and a therapy-inducing trauma.

Labor issues are another concern. Many haunted attractions rely on seasonal workers, often paying low wages for physically and emotionally demanding work. There have been calls for better treatment and compensation for haunted house actors and staff. Because apparently, minimum wage isn't quite enough compensation for having to pretend to be a demon every night.

Cultural sensitivity is another challenge. Some haunted attractions have faced criticism for incorporating offensive stereotypes or insensitive portrayals of mental illness. The industry is grappling with how to provide scares without crossing lines of taste or respect. It turns out, there's more to fear than fear itself – there's also the fear of bad PR.

Looking to the future, we might see personalized scares tailored to your specific fears. Imagine a haunted house that knows you're terrified of public speaking and confronts you with a room full of expectant audience members. It's like Facebook's targeted ads, but for your deepest anxieties.

We could also see fully immersive environments using advanced haptic technology and environmental controls. Think "Westworld," but with more chainsaws and fewer existential crises about the nature of reality. Actually, scratch that – probably about the same number of existential crises.

There's even talk of citywide haunted experiences where the scares could come at any time, anywhere. Because what could possibly go wrong with blurring the lines between a controlled haunted attraction and everyday life? Paranoia has never been so fun!

As we emerge from our tour of the haunted attraction industry (hopefully with all our limbs intact and only minor psychological scarring), it's clear that our love affair with recreational terror is far from over. From the humble beginnings of fairground ghost trains to the high-tech horror shows of today, haunted attractions have evolved to meet our ever-growing appetite for controlled fear.

These attractions offer us a unique opportunity to confront our fears, challenge our limits, and scream our heads off in a safe environment. They're a testament to human creativity, our complex relationship with fear, and our apparently boundless capacity for paying money to have the wits scared out of us.

So the next time you find yourself in a haunted house, heart pounding as you turn a dark corner, take a moment to appreciate the artistry and psychology at work. Remember that behind every zombie, ghost, and chainsaw-wielding maniac is a team of dedicated professionals working hard to ensure you have the worst time of your life... in the best possible way.

And if all else fails, just remember the golden rule of haunted houses: you don't have to be the fastest runner in your group. You just have to be faster than the slowest person. Happy haunting!

Chapter 5: Halloween Goes Hollywood The Fright Film Phenomenon

Lights, camera, action... scream! Welcome to the world of Halloween-themed movies, where things go bump in the night, teenagers make questionable decisions, and masked killers have more lives than a cat sanctuary. From the campy classics of yesteryear to the psychological thrillers of today, Halloween movies have become as much a part of the holiday as candy corn and questionable costume choices. So grab your popcorn (and maybe a security blanket), as we dive into the thrilling, chilling world of Halloween cinema.

To understand how Halloween became so intertwined with the world of film, we need to take a step back and look at the early days of cinema. The horror genre has been with us almost since the invention of moving pictures. In fact, some film historians argue that the first-ever narrative film, Georges Méliès' "Le Manoir du Diable" (The House of the Devil) from 1896, was a horror movie. It featured such terrifying spectacles as a bat turning into Mephistopheles and a woman turning into a skeleton. Truly the stuff of nightmares... if you were easily frightened and living in the 19th century.

As cinema evolved, so did its capacity to scare audiences. The German Expressionist movement of the 1920s gave us classics like "Nosferatu" (1922) and "The Cabinet of Dr. Caligari" (1920), which established many of the visual tropes we still associate with horror today. Because nothing says "spooky" quite like extreme angles, heavy shadows, and actors wearing more makeup than a drag queen at a glitter factory.

But it wasn't until the 1930s that Hollywood really got into the horror game, with Universal Studios leading the charge. Films like "Dracula" (1931), "Frankenstein" (1931), and "The Mummy" (1932) not only terrified audiences but also established horror as a viable and profitable genre. They also gave us some of the most iconic Halloween costumes of all time. Thank you, Universal, for ensuring that every Halloween party for the next century would have at least one person wrapped in toilet paper pretending to be a mummy.

While these early horror films weren't specifically tied to Halloween, they laid the groundwork for the holiday's association with all things spooky and scary. As Halloween celebrations in America grew more elaborate throughout the 20th century, the holiday and the horror genre became increasingly intertwined.

This connection was cemented in 1978 with the release of John Carpenter's "Halloween." This low-budget slasher film, featuring the now-iconic Michael Myers, wasn't the first horror movie set on Halloween (that honor goes to the 1944 film "The Ghost of Frankenstein"), but it was certainly the most influential. "Halloween" not only launched a franchise that's still going strong today but also kicked off the golden age of slasher films. Suddenly, every holiday was fair game for a horror movie. Valentine's Day? "My Bloody Valentine." Christmas? "Silent Night, Deadly Night." Arbor Day? Okay, maybe not every holiday.

The success of "Halloween" spawned numerous imitators and helped establish many of the tropes we now associate with horror films: the final girl, the unstoppable killer, and the shocking twist that the killer isn't actually dead (surprise!). It also solidified the connection between the Halloween holiday and horror cinema in the public imagination.

The 1980s saw an explosion of slasher films, many of which have become Halloween viewing staples. "Friday the 13th" (1980) taught us to be wary of summer camps and hockey masks. "A Nightmare on Elm Street" (1984) made us think twice about falling asleep. And "Child's Play" (1988) ensured that a whole generation would eye their dolls with suspicion.

These films, with their mix of scares, gore, and often unintentional humor, became a central part of Halloween culture. Watching them became a Halloween tradition for many, a way to get into the spooky spirit of the season. They also provided a wealth of costume ideas. Suddenly, every Halloween party had at least one Freddy Krueger, complete with striped sweater and garishly burned face. Because nothing says "festive holiday gathering" quite like dressing as a child murderer, right?

But it wasn't all blood and guts. The 80s also gave us some lighter Halloween fare...

The 1980s also saw the rise of horror-comedies that blended scares with laughs. Films like "Ghostbusters" (1984) and "Beetlejuice" (1988) brought supernatural elements into the mainstream, making them more accessible (and marketable) to a wider audience.

These films showed that Halloween-themed movies didn't have to be pure horror. They could be funny, quirky, and even family-friendly while still embracing the spooky aesthetic of the holiday. "Ghostbusters" in particular had a massive cultural impact, spawning a multimedia franchise that's still going strong today. It also gave us the eternally quotable line "Who you gonna call?", which has been the bane of customer service representatives ever since.

"Beetlejuice" took a different approach, embracing the weird and grotesque in a way that was more quirky than scary. It turned the afterlife into a bizarre bureaucracy and made death seem like just another inconvenience. It also launched a thousand Lydia Deetz goth girl costumes and made us all a little wary of saying anyone's name three times.

As we moved into the 1990s, the Halloween movie landscape began to shift. The slasher genre, which had dominated the 80s, was starting to feel a bit stale. Audiences had seen one too many masked killers and final girls. It was time for something new.

Enter "Scream" (1996). This meta-horror film, directed by slasher veteran Wes Craven, breathed new life into the genre by being self-aware. The characters in "Scream" had seen all the same horror movies we had, and they knew the rules. Of course, that didn't stop them from breaking those rules and getting killed anyway, but hey, at least they were genre-savvy victims.

"Scream" sparked a revival of the slasher genre and inspired a new wave of teen-oriented horror films. Suddenly, every horror movie had to have a cast of impossibly attractive young people making quippy remarks while being stalked by a killer. It was like "Dawson's Creek," but with more stabbing and fewer SAT words.

The 90s also saw a rise in horror-themed kids' movies perfect for Halloween viewing. Films like "Hocus Pocus" (1993) and "The Nightmare Before Christmas" (1993) brought spooky themes to younger audiences. "Hocus Pocus" in particular has become a Halloween classic, enjoyed by those who saw it as kids and a new generation discovering it on endless cable TV reruns. It also ensured that no one would ever look at a vacuum cleaner the same way again.

As we entered the 2000s, the Halloween movie landscape continued to evolve. The found footage genre, pioneered by "The Blair Witch Project" in 1999, exploded in popularity. Suddenly, every horror movie was trying to convince us that it was actual footage of real events. Because apparently, in the world of found footage films, the first instinct of anyone encountering a supernatural threat is to keep filming no matter what.

This era also saw the rise of horror franchises that became Halloween viewing staples. The "Saw" series, which kicked off in 2004, gave us seven straight years of increasingly elaborate deathtraps and convoluted plotlines. It also made us all a little more appreciative of our limbs.

The "Paranormal Activity" franchise, starting in 2007, combined the found footage trend with haunted house tropes. It taught us that ghosts really love to slam doors and drag people out of bed. It also made us all a little more suspicious of security cameras and why they always seem to glitch at the most inopportune moments.

Torture porn, a charming subgenre that emphasized graphic violence and gore, also gained prominence in this era with films like "Hostel" (2005). These movies pushed the boundaries of what audiences could stomach, both literally and figuratively. They also made us all a little more wary of staying in sketchy Eastern European hostels. Thanks for that, Eli Roth.

In recent years, we've seen the rise of what some critics call "elevated horror." These are films that use horror elements to explore deeper themes and social issues. Movies like "Get Out" (2017), "Hereditary" (2018), and "The Babadook" (2014) have shown that horror can be both terrifying and thought-provoking.

These films have become popular Halloween viewing choices for those who want their scares with a side of social commentary. "Get Out" used horror tropes to explore racism in America. "Hereditary" delved into family trauma and grief. And "The Babadook" gave us a monster that was also a poignant metaphor for depression... and then became an unexpected LGBTQ+ icon, because the internet is a strange and wonderful place.

This trend has helped legitimize horror in the eyes of critics and awards bodies. It's no longer just the genre of cheap thrills and cheaper fake blood. Now it's the genre of cheap thrills, cheaper fake blood, and incisive social commentary. Progress!

The rise of streaming services has had a huge impact on how we consume Halloween-themed movies. No longer do we have to wait for the annual TV showing of our favorite spooky film or trek to the video store to rent a scary movie. Now, with the click of a button, we can access a vast library of Halloween-appropriate viewing.

This has led to some interesting trends. For one, it's easier than ever for older Halloween movies to find new audiences. Films that might have faded into obscurity are getting second lives as streaming favorites. It's also allowed for the creation of Halloween-themed content specifically for streaming platforms.

Netflix, for example, has had great success with its "Fear Street" trilogy, based on R.L. Stine's books. These films, released in quick succession, became a Halloween event in their own right. They also proved that you can never go wrong with a healthy dose of 90s nostalgia and a killer soundtrack.

The streaming era has also given new life to horror TV series. Shows like "Stranger Things," "American Horror Story," and "The Haunting of Hill House" have become Halloween viewing staples, offering long-form scares perfect for binge-watching on chilly October nights.

It's hard to overstate the impact that Halloween-themed movies have had on the holiday itself. These films have shaped how we celebrate Halloween, influencing everything from costume choices to decoration trends.

Think about it: how many Michael Myers or Ghostface costumes do you see every Halloween? How many people decorate their houses to look like the Addams Family mansion or the Sanderson sisters' cottage from "Hocus Pocus"? Halloween movies have given us a shared visual language for the holiday, a set of references and images that we all understand.

These films have also influenced how we think about fear and what scares us. They've taken our primal fears – of the dark, of death, of the unknown – and given them shape and form. They've created new monsters for us to fear and new scenarios to dread. Thanks to "Jaws," we're afraid to go in the water. Thanks to "The Blair Witch Project," we're wary of camping in unfamiliar woods. And thanks to "Final Destination," we're suspicious of... well, pretty much everything.

But perhaps most importantly, Halloween movies have given us a way to confront these fears in a safe, controlled environment. They allow us to experience fear and anxiety vicariously, from the safety of our couches. It's like a fear inoculation – a small, manageable dose of fright to help us deal with the real fears we face in our daily lives.

As we look to the future, it's clear that Halloween-themed movies aren't going anywhere. If anything, they're likely to become even more central to how we celebrate the holiday. But what might these future fright films look like?

One trend we're likely to see continue is the blending of horror with other genres. We've already seen horror-comedies and horror-dramas. Could horror-musicals be the next big thing? "Sweeney Todd" has already shown us that singing and slashing can go hand in hand.

We're also likely to see more films that use horror elements to explore social issues. As society grapples with challenges like climate change, political polarization, and technological advancement, horror films will likely reflect these anxieties. Get ready for eco-horror, political horror, and AI horror. Because apparently, reality isn't scary enough on its own.

Virtual and augmented reality technologies could also change how we experience Halloween movies. Imagine a horror film where you're not just watching the protagonist flee from the monster – you are the protagonist. It could add a whole new dimension to the concept of an immersive cinematic experience. Just make sure you have a change of pants ready.

As we reach the end of our journey through the world of Halloween cinema, it's clear that the relationship between the holiday and horror movies is a symbiotic one. Halloween provides the perfect backdrop for scary stories, and these stories, in turn, have shaped how we celebrate the holiday.

From the early days of Universal monsters to the meta-horror of "Scream," from the family-friendly frights of "Hocus Pocus" to the psychological terror of "Hereditary," Halloween movies have given us a vast and varied pantheon of fears to choose from. They've made us scream, laugh, and occasionally question our life choices ("Why am I watching this alone in the dark?").

These films have become more than just entertainment – they're an integral part of our Halloween traditions. They're the stories we tell to scare ourselves, the images we reference in our costumes and decorations, the shared experiences that bring us together in communal fear and excitement.

So this Halloween, as you settle in for your annual viewing of "Halloween" (the movie, not the holiday – though I suppose you could watch the movie "Halloween" on Halloween, which would be very meta), take a moment to appreciate the rich cinematic history behind your fear. And remember – if you hear a strange noise, or if the car won't start, or if you're tempted to investigate that dark basement alone... maybe don't. After all, you've seen enough Halloween movies to know better.

Chapter 6: Witch, Please
Feminism, Paganism, and Halloween

Now, if you've been paying attention to Halloween trends lately, you might have noticed something peculiar. Witches are everywhere. And no, I'm not talking about that coven of suburban moms who drink wine and call it "witch's brew" while discussing their latest MLM scheme. I'm talking about a full-blown witch renaissance.

But before we dive into the modern magical madness, let's take a moment to appreciate the sheer absurdity of witch history. Picture this: it's the 15th century, and you're a woman who knows a bit too much about herbs or has a cat that's a little too sassy. Congratulations! You're now the prime suspect in every unexplained village mishap, from spoiled milk to impotent husbands. It's like being the Karen of the Middle Ages, except instead of asking to speak to the manager, you get dunked in a river.

The witch hunts of Europe and colonial America were no laughing matter, though. Thousands of people, mostly women, were tortured and killed under accusations of witchcraft. It was a horrific period that demonstrated how easily fear, misogyny, and mass hysteria could combine into a perfect storm of injustice. It's like if Twitter became a legal system, but with more burning at the stake and fewer memes.

Fast forward to today, and witches have gone from being the most feared members of society to being, well, still feared, but in a "Yass, queen, slay!" kind of way. The image of the witch has been reclaimed faster than you can say "Hocus Pocus." And speaking of "Hocus Pocus," let's take a moment to appreciate how that movie single-handedly made a generation of kids think that virgin-shaming and cat murder were integral parts of Halloween. Thanks, Disney!

But the modern witch image isn't just about entertainment. It's become a powerful symbol in feminism and pop culture. The witch represents everything that patriarchal societies have long feared in women: independence, knowledge, sexuality, and power. It's like a Venn diagram where "things witches do" and "things that scare insecure men" is just a single circle.

Feminist scholars have embraced the witch as a figure of female empowerment. After all, what's more empowering than being able to hex your enemies and turn men into toads? It's the ultimate "girl power" fantasy, except instead of forming a pop group and singing about friendship, you're forming a coven and singing about the downfall of the patriarchy. Same energy, really.

This reclamation of the witch image has led to some fascinating cultural phenomena. Take, for example, the rise of "witch aesthetics" on social media. Suddenly, everyone's Instagram feed is full of crystal collections, tarot cards, and enough plants to make a botanical garden jealous. It's like cottagecore met The Craft in a dark alley, and the result was a million "witch kits" sold on Etsy.

But it's not all aesthetic and no substance. Modern paganism and witchcraft have seen a significant resurgence, with many people finding spiritual fulfillment in these ancient practices. And before you scoff, remember that believing in the power of crystals is no weirder than believing that a wafer turns into the body of Christ. At least with crystals, you get some nice home decor out of the deal.

The connection between modern paganism and Halloween is stronger than ever. While Halloween has its roots in the Celtic festival of Samhain, many contemporary pagans and witches celebrate it as one of the most important holidays in their spiritual calendar. It's a time when the veil between worlds is said to be thinnest, allowing for communication with the spirit realm. So, the next time you're bobbing for apples, remember that you might be accidentally participating in an ancient spiritual ritual. Or you might just be getting a mouthful of backwash. Either way, it's a magical experience.

Now, let's talk about the elephant in the room, or should I say, the broomstick in the closet: WitchTok. Yes, that's right, witchcraft has invaded TikTok, and the result is exactly as chaotic as you'd expect. WitchTok is a corner of the app where users share spells, rituals, and enough dramatic music to make a Broadway producer jealous. It's like if Harry Potter and a VSCO girl had a baby, and that baby was really into manifestation and charging crystals under the full moon.

WitchTok has become so popular that it's sparked debates within the witchcraft community about the authenticity and ethics of sharing magical practices on social media. Some argue that it's making witchcraft more accessible, while others worry that it's reducing complex spiritual practices to trendy 60-second videos. It's the magical equivalent of learning brain surgery from a YouTube tutorial. Sure, you might learn something, but do you really want to risk it?

But regardless of where you stand on the WitchTok debate, there's no denying that technology has changed the face of modern witchcraft. Gone are the days when aspiring witches had to seek out obscure occult bookshops or join secretive covens. Now, you can order a complete witch starter kit on Amazon Prime and be hexing your ex by dinnertime. It's convenience culture meets the occult, and it's about as 21st century as you can get.

This digital age of witchcraft has led to some truly bizarre products and services. Want a personally tailored spell sent to your inbox every full moon? There's a subscription service for that. Interested in a AI-generated tarot reading? There's an app for that. Curious about what your cat's astrological sign means for your love life? There's probably a podcast about that, and if there isn't, give it a week.

The commercialization of witchcraft might seem at odds with its countercultural roots, but it's not a new phenomenon. Occult and New Age shops have been around for decades, selling everything from crystal balls to pre-packaged love spells. The difference now is the scale and accessibility. You no longer need to be "in the know" to access these products; you just need an internet connection and a willingness to explain some very strange packages to your mailman.

But amidst all this magical mayhem, it's important to remember the very real and often overlooked spiritual practices that form the backbone of modern paganism and witchcraft. Many practitioners take their beliefs and rituals seriously, finding genuine meaning and community in these traditions. It's easy to laugh at the idea of dancing naked in the moonlight, but for some people, it's a profound spiritual experience. And let's be honest, is it any weirder than eating a cracker and pretending it's the body of your deity? Religion is weird, folks. Let's just embrace it.

The intersection of feminism, paganism, and Halloween has created a cultural cauldron that's bubbling with possibilities. It's a space where women (and men, and non-binary folks – let's not forget that modern witchcraft is often queer-friendly) can explore power, spirituality, and identity outside of traditional patriarchal structures. It's like a spiritual Choose Your Own Adventure, but with more candles and fewer cave trolls.

This witch renaissance has also sparked important conversations about cultural appropriation and the commodification of spiritual practices. As with any trend, there's a risk of surface-level engagement that doesn't respect the depth and complexity of the traditions involved. It's great that more people are interested in these practices, but maybe don't call yourself a "bruja" if your only exposure to Latin American culture is that one time you got really into Shakira.

The popularity of witchcraft and paganism around Halloween has also led to some interesting clashes with more traditional Halloween celebrations. While some embrace the spooky season as a time to openly practice their craft, others find themselves explaining for the hundredth time that no, they don't worship Satan, and no, they can't make your crush fall in love with you. It's a delicate balance between reveling in the witchy vibes of the season and educating people about the realities of modern pagan practices.

And let's not forget the annual outcry from certain religious groups who see Halloween – and especially its more pagan elements – as a threat to their beliefs. It's a tale as old as time: one person's harmless fun is another person's highway to hell. But here's the thing: if your faith can be shaken by a plastic cauldron and some fake spiderwebs, maybe the problem isn't Halloween.

As we wrap up this magical mystery tour of modern witchcraft, it's worth considering what this trend says about our society. The resurgence of interest in witchcraft and paganism could be seen as a response to the uncertainties of modern life. In a world where traditional institutions are increasingly questioned, where climate change looms large, and where political systems seem to be failing us, is it any wonder that people are turning to alternative sources of meaning and power?

Witchcraft offers a sense of control in an uncontrollable world. Can't afford health insurance? Try a healing crystal! Worried about the economy? Light a green candle for prosperity! Frustrated with the patriarchy? There's a hex for that! It's not a solution to systemic problems, of course, but it does provide a sense of agency and community that many people find lacking in their lives.

So this Halloween, as you don your pointy hat and practice your best cackle, take a moment to appreciate the complex history and modern significance of the witch image. Whether you're a dedicated practitioner of the craft or just someone who really likes black cats and mini cauldrons, you're participating in a centuries-old tradition of challenging the status quo and embracing the mysterious.

And who knows? Maybe there's more magic in the world than we give it credit for. After all, in a universe where quantum physics exists and platypuses are a real animal, is it really so hard to believe in a little witchcraft? So go ahead, stir that cauldron, light those candles, and embrace your inner witch. Just maybe don't try to fly on a broomstick. That's what we have budget airlines for.

In conclusion, the modern witch is a complex figure, embodying feminism, spirituality, rebellion, and a really great excuse to wear all black. She's come a long way from the feared outcast of medieval villages to the empowered icon of today. So the next time someone calls you a witch, don't get offended. Just smile mysteriously and say, "Witch, please." And then turn them into a newt. I'm kidding, of course. Or am I?

Chapter 7: Jack-o'-Lantern's Carbon Footprint
The Environmental Impact of Halloween

Alright, gather 'round, boys and ghouls, because we're about to carve into a topic scarier than any haunted house or horror movie: the environmental impact of Halloween. That's right, we're going green with our orange and black, and let me tell you, it's not a pretty picture. It turns out our beloved spooky season is leaving behind more than just fond memories and candy wrappers – it's leaving a carbon footprint big enough to make Bigfoot jealous.

Let's start with everyone's favorite Halloween tradition: pumpkin carving. Every year, millions of pumpkins are grown, harvested, transported, and sold for the sole purpose of being turned into gap-toothed, candle-lit decorations. And what happens to these orange orbs of festivity after October 31st? Well, if they're lucky, they might end up in a compost bin. But more often than not, they're tossed in the trash faster than you can say "The Great Pumpkin, Charlie Brown."

In the U.S. alone, it's estimated that about 1.3 billion pounds of pumpkin end up in landfills each year. That's more wasted pumpkin than you'd get if you gave the entire population of China a slice of pumpkin pie. And when these pumpkins decompose in landfills, they release methane, a greenhouse gas that's about 28 times more potent than carbon dioxide. It's like we're literally carving jack-o'-lantern faces into the ozone layer.

But before you start feeling too guilty about your pumpkin-carving habits, let me assure you that this is just the tip of the melting iceberg when it comes to Halloween's environmental impact. Let's talk about costumes, shall we? The fashion industry is already notorious for its environmental impact, but Halloween costumes take it to a whole new level of wasteful.

Every year, millions of people buy costumes that they'll wear exactly once before relegating them to the back of the closet or, more likely, the trash. These costumes are often made from synthetic materials like polyester, which is basically just a fancy word for plastic. And we all know how great plastic is for the environment, right? (That was sarcasm, in case you couldn't tell. Plastic is terrible for the environment. It's like the mustache-twirling villain in the environmental melodrama of our lives.)

The problem with these costumes isn't just that they're made from non-biodegradable materials. It's also the fact that they're often cheaply made and designed to fall apart faster than a vampire in sunlight. It's fast fashion at its spookiest – costumes that are worn once and then discarded, contributing to the mountains of textile waste that plague our planet.

And let's not forget about all the accessories that go along with these costumes. Plastic fangs, rubber masks, synthetic wigs – it's like we're trying to create a landfill version of Madame Tussauds. These items aren't just non-biodegradable; they're often toxic, containing chemicals that can leach into the soil and water. It's enough to make you want to dress up as an environmental disaster for Halloween – oh wait, we're already doing that collectively.

But wait, there's more! (And no, this isn't a strange kind of infomercial for environmentally friendly Halloween products, although maybe it should be.) Let's talk about decorations. From plastic skeletons to synthetic cobwebs, the average Halloween decor is about as eco-friendly as a coal-powered power plant.

Many of these decorations are designed to be disposable, used for one season and then tossed out. And even if you do keep them, let's be honest – how many years can a plastic jack-o'-lantern really last before it starts to look less "spooky" and more "sad"? It's a cycle of consumption and waste that would make even the most hardened capitalist ghost say, "Boo-hoo."

And don't even get me started on Halloween lights. These energy-sucking strings of orange and purple are like Christmas lights' evil twin. They're often left on for hours, contributing to unnecessary energy consumption. It's like we're trying to signal aliens with our Halloween spirit, but all we're really doing is signaling our disregard for energy conservation.

Now, I know what you're thinking. "But what about trick-or-treating? Surely that innocent tradition of children extorting candy from their neighbors can't be bad for the environment?" Oh, my sweet summer child (or should I say, my innocent Halloween goblin?), let me introduce you to the horrors of individually wrapped candy.

Each year, millions of tiny candy bars and lollipops are distributed, each one wrapped in its own little plastic cocoon. It's like we're trying to preserve these sweets for future archaeologists to discover. "Ah yes," they'll say, "this must be from the era when humans decided that each piece of candy needed its own protective forcefield."

The problem isn't just the wrappers themselves, although those are bad enough. It's also the fact that these wrappers are too small to be recycled in most facilities. So even if you're the type of person who diligently separates your recyclables (and if you are, good for you, you eco-warrior), those tiny candy wrappers are still destined for the landfill.

But before you decide to cancel Halloween altogether and spend October 31st sitting in the dark to conserve energy, let's talk about some solutions. Because believe it or not, it is possible to have a spooky good time without treating the environment like it's the villain in a slasher film.

First up: pumpkins. If you're going to carve a jack-o'-lantern (and let's face it, it's not really Halloween without one), consider composting it afterward. And if you're not into composting, at least consider eating it. Pumpkin pie, pumpkin soup, pumpkin spice lattes – the possibilities are endless. Just maybe don't try to eat the one that's been sitting on your porch for two weeks. That's a different kind of horror story.

When it comes to costumes, consider the radical idea of... reusing them. I know, I know, it's a shocking concept in our throwaway culture. But hear me out. What if, instead of buying a new plastic-wrapped costume each year, you created a costume from things you already own? Or, even wilder, what if you swapped costumes with friends? It's like The Sisterhood of the Traveling Pants, but spookier.

For those who insist on buying new costumes, there are increasingly eco-friendly options available. Costumes made from organic cotton, bamboo, or recycled materials are becoming more common. Yes, they might be more expensive than the $19.99 polyester nightmare from the Halloween superstore, but consider it an investment in both your Halloween future and the planet's.

As for decorations, the same principles apply. Reuse what you have, create decorations from natural or recyclable materials, or invest in high-quality decorations that will last for years. And if you must have Halloween lights, consider solar-powered options or at least use LED bulbs. Your electricity bill will thank you, even if the ghosts and goblins don't.

When it comes to trick-or-treating, consider handing out treats that aren't individually wrapped. Fruits, small toys, or homemade treats can be good alternatives – although be prepared for some skeptical parents if you go the homemade route. Years of urban legends about razor blades in apples have made people understandably wary of non-packaged Halloween treats. Thanks a lot, moral panic of the 1970s.

Some communities have started organizing Halloween costume swaps, decoration exchanges, and even pumpkin composting programs. It's like a farmers' market, but for Halloween stuff. And let's be honest, browsing through other people's old Halloween decorations is probably more entertaining than most haunted houses.

There are also some truly innovative eco-friendly Halloween initiatives popping up. Some towns have started "Pumpkin Smash" events, where people bring their old jack-o'-lanterns to be composted en masse. It's like a post-Halloween party where the guests of honor are rotting vegetables. Fun for the whole family!

Other communities have organized Halloween cleanup events, where volunteers dress up in costumes and pick up litter. It's a great way to combine community service with the Halloween spirit. Plus, there's something oddly satisfying about seeing Superman pick up candy wrappers or Elsa from Frozen collecting discarded decorations.

Some eco-conscious Halloween enthusiasts have even started creating their own biodegradable Halloween decorations. Think pumpkins carved with messages about climate change, or skeletons made from compostable materials. It's like if Greta Thunberg decided to open a Halloween store.

The point is, with a little creativity and mindfulness, it's possible to celebrate Halloween without treating the environment like it's expendable. After all, what's the point of dressing up as a post-apocalyptic survivor if we're actually creating the apocalypse with our Halloween habits?

So this Halloween, as you're deciding between dressing as a sexy nurse or a scary clown (or a scary sexy nurse clown, no judgment here), take a moment to consider the environmental impact of your choices. Because the scariest thing about Halloween shouldn't be what it's doing to our planet.

Remember, every little bit helps. You might not single-handedly save the world by composting your pumpkin, but you'll be contributing to a larger movement towards a more sustainable Halloween. And who knows? Maybe your eco-friendly Halloween efforts will inspire others. It could be the start of a green Halloween revolution. Viva la Jack-o'-lantern!

In the end, Halloween is about fun, creativity, and community. There's no reason we can't maintain those values while also being kinder to our environment. So go forth, my eco-warriors of the night, and show the world that green is the new orange and black. And if anyone gives you grief about your sustainable Halloween choices, just tell them you're dressed as the ghost of Halloween future – here to warn them about the environmental horrors to come if we don't change our ways.

Chapter 8: Boo-hoo Halloween Controversies and Moral Panics

Alright, folks, strap in, because we're about to dive into the drama-filled world of Halloween controversies and moral panics. It's like a soap opera, but with more fake blood and fewer evil twins (although who knows, maybe the evil twins are just wearing really good costumes).

Let's start with the granddaddy of all Halloween panics: the Satanic Panic of the 1980s and early 1990s. For those of you too young to remember (or those who've blocked it out), this was a period when a significant portion of America became convinced that Satanic cults were lurking around every corner, waiting to snatch children and sacrifice them in elaborate rituals. And naturally, Halloween was seen as prime time for these supposed Satanic shenanigans.

The Satanic Panic led to some truly bizarre claims about Halloween. People were warned about poisoned candy, apples with razor blades, and roving gangs of Satanists looking to kidnap trick-or-treaters. It was like the plot of a bad horror movie, except people actually believed it. Schools cancelled Halloween celebrations, parents kept their kids indoors, and the sale of candy x-ray machines skyrocketed. Yes, you heard that right – candy x-ray machines. Because nothing says "Happy Halloween" like treating your child's trick-or-treat haul like suspicious luggage at the airport.

The funny thing is, despite years of panic and countless news reports, there has never been a single verified case of a stranger poisoning Halloween candy. Not one. The razor blade in the apple thing? Also largely a myth. It turns out the biggest danger on Halloween is probably tripping over your own costume or eating so much candy you make yourself sick. But hey, why let facts get in the way of a good moral panic?

The Satanic Panic eventually faded, but it left behind a legacy of Halloween fear-mongering that persists to this day. Every year, like clockwork, some local news station will run a story about the "hidden dangers" of Halloween. It's like they have a dartboard of potential threats – sex offenders, drug-laced candy, kidnapping – and they just throw a dart to decide what to scare parents about this year.

But the controversies surrounding Halloween aren't just about imaginary Satanists and poisoned Snickers bars. Oh no, we're much more creative than that in our moral outrage. Let's talk about the great Halloween-in-schools debate, shall we?

Every year, schools across the country grapple with the question of whether and how to celebrate Halloween. On one side, you have the "It's just harmless fun!" crowd. On the other, you have a mix of religious objectors, cultural sensitivity advocates, and people who just really hate fun. It's like a battle royale, but instead of fighting to the death, they're fighting over whether little Timmy can wear his Superman costume to math class.

The arguments against Halloween celebrations in schools range from the religious (some see it as a pagan holiday) to the practical (it's disruptive to learning) to the inclusive (not everyone celebrates Halloween). And you know what? Some of these arguments have merit. It's true that Halloween has pagan roots, it can be disruptive, and not everyone celebrates it.

But here's the thing: by that logic, we should probably cancel every holiday celebration in schools. Christmas? Religious. Valentine's Day? Not everyone dates. Presidents' Day? Political. Before you know it, kids will be left with nothing to celebrate except standardized test day. And let me tell you, no one's dressing up for that.

The Halloween-in-schools debate has led to some truly creative compromises. Some schools have "fall festivals" instead of Halloween parties. It's basically the same thing, but with more corn mazes and fewer vampires. Other schools allow costumes but ban anything "too scary" or "culturally insensitive." Good luck defining those terms. Is a zombie culturally insensitive to the undead community?

Speaking of culturally insensitive costumes, let's dive into that particularly spicy cauldron of controversy. Every year, without fail, someone makes headlines for wearing a costume that's about as culturally sensitive as Christopher Columbus at a Native American heritage celebration.

From celebrities wearing blackface (seriously, how is this still happening?) to frat boys dressing up as offensive stereotypes, it seems like some people use Halloween as an excuse to let their racist flag fly. It's like they think a costume gives them a free pass to be terrible. News flash: dressing up as a "Mexican bandit" or a "geisha girl" isn't clever or funny. It's just racist. And no, adding the word "sexy" in front of it doesn't make it better. "Sexy racist" is not a look anyone should be going for.

The debate over offensive costumes has led to some interesting cultural conversations. It's forced us to examine the line between appreciation and appropriation, to think about the impact of our choices, and to consider perspectives we might not have considered before. It's also led to a lot of angry Facebook posts and Twitter wars, but hey, that's just the world we live in now.

Some universities and workplaces have started issuing guidelines about appropriate Halloween costumes. And predictably, this has led to cries of "political correctness gone mad!" from certain quarters. Because apparently, for some people, the right to dress up as an offensive stereotype is the hill they want to die on. It's like the costume version of "Don't tread on me," except instead of a snake on the flag, it's a white guy in a sombrero.

But the Halloween controversies don't stop there. Oh no, we're just getting started. Let's talk about the great sexy costume debate, shall we? Every year, like clockwork, someone writes an op-ed bemoaning the prevalence of "sexy" costumes for women. "Why does everything have to be sexy?" they cry. "Where are the non-sexy options?"

And you know what? They have a point. The options for women's Halloween costumes often seem to be limited to "sexy profession" (sexy nurse, sexy teacher, sexy accountant – okay, maybe not that last one), "sexy animal" (sexy cat, sexy mouse, sexy platypus – okay, I made that one up), or "sexy fictional character" (sexy Elsa, sexy Wonder Woman, sexy Shrek – again, I hope I made that one up).

But here's the thing: while it's absolutely true that women should have more non-sexy options (and that "sexy" shouldn't be the default), the pearl-clutching over sexy costumes often veers into slut-shaming territory faster than you can say "trick or treat." The problem isn't that sexy costumes exist – it's that they're often the only option presented to women, and that women are judged harshly whether they choose to wear them or not.

The sexy costume debate is really just a microcosm of larger societal issues around women's bodies and choices. It's like all our cultural baggage gets stuffed into a sexy nurse costume and paraded down the street on October 31st.

But wait, there's more! (Why does that sound like another weird infomercial? Are we selling Halloween controversies now?) Let's talk about the intersection of Halloween and religion, a combination about as peaceful and harmonious as oil and water at a candlelit dinner.

Some religious groups have long taken issue with Halloween, seeing it as a celebration of evil or the occult. This has led to some... interesting alternatives. "Harvest festivals" that are totally not Halloween wink wink. "Jesus Ween" (yes, that's a real thing) where kids dress up as biblical characters and hand out bibles instead of candy. Because nothing says "fun holiday for children" like being handed religious literature instead of chocolate.

On the flip side, some Pagans and Wiccans have expressed frustration with the commercialization and secularization of what they consider a sacred holiday. It's like if Christmas was only about Santa and had nothing to do with Jesus... oh wait.

The result is a bizarre situation where some people think Halloween is too pagan, some think it's not pagan enough, and the rest of us are just trying to figure out how to get the fake blood stains out of our sexy accounting costume.

But perhaps the most unexpected Halloween controversy in recent years came courtesy of our old friend, COVID-19. That's right, even a global pandemic couldn't resist getting in on the Halloween drama.

In 2020, as the pandemic raged, Halloween became an unexpected battleground in the culture wars. Public health officials urged people to skip trick-or-treating and large Halloween gatherings. Some listened. Others... didn't. It was like watching a real-time experiment in risk assessment and social responsibility, with candy corn as the control variable.

Creative solutions abounded. People made candy chutes to deliver treats from a safe distance. Drive-through haunted houses became a thing. Zoom costume parties tested the limits of both internet bandwidth and human patience. It was a masterclass in adaptation, with a side of existential dread.

But it also highlighted existing social divides. Those who insisted on traditional trick-or-treating were labeled as selfish and irresponsible by some, while they accused the stay-at-homers of being paranoid and joyless. It was like the Halloween version of the mask debate, but with more fake spiderwebs.

As we emerge from one pandemic (fingers crossed there isn't another one), it's unclear what long-term effects it will have on Halloween celebrations. Will people embrace traditional activities with renewed enthusiasm? Will some of the pandemic-era adaptations stick around? Will we all just be too tired to celebrate and decide to hibernate through October instead?

Looking at all these controversies, it's easy to wonder: why do we care so much? Why does a holiday ostensibly for children provoke so much adult hand-wringing and debate?

Part of it, I think, is that Halloween serves as a kind of pressure release valve for society. It's the one night a year when many of our normal rules are suspended. We dress up as someone (or something) else. We embrace the spooky and macabre. We let our kids take candy from strangers, for crying out loud!

So when we argue about Halloween, we're often really arguing about larger social issues. Debates about costumes become debates about race and gender. Arguments about trick-or-treating become arguments about safety and community. Controversies over Halloween in schools become proxy wars for larger battles over religion in public life.

In a way, Halloween holds up a mirror to our society, showing us our fears, our values, and our contradictions. It's just that the mirror is one of those funhouse ones that makes everything look a bit distorted and spooky.

So the next time you find yourself in a heated debate about whether it's okay for your kid to dress up as Moana, or whether fake blood is an appropriate decoration for a second-grade classroom, remember: it's not really about Halloween. It's about who we are as a society and who we want to be.

And on that profound note, let's move on to our next chapter, where we'll explore how technology is changing the face of Halloween. Spoiler alert: it involves more screens and hopefully fewer toilet paper mummies.

Chapter 9: Ghosts in the Machine Technology and the Future of Halloween

Welcome to the future of Halloween, where the ghosts are digital, the pumpkins are 3D-printed, and your costume is more likely to need Wi-Fi than fake blood. That's right, we're diving into the world of high-tech haunting, where Silicon Valley meets Transylvania.

Let's start with virtual and augmented reality Halloween experiences. Remember when a haunted house was just some guy in a rubber mask jumping out from behind a curtain? Well, those days are as dead as the zombies you're now fighting in your VR headset.

VR haunted houses are becoming increasingly popular, offering experiences that range from mildly spooky to "I think I just peed a little." The advantage? You can have a heart-pounding horror experience without ever leaving your living room. The disadvantage? You might accidentally punch your cat while flailing around in terror. Sorry, Fluffy, but in my defense, you did look a lot like a virtual zombie in that moment.

Augmented reality is also getting in on the Halloween action. Imagine pointing your phone at your boring old house and seeing it transformed into a creepy haunted mansion. Or watching skeletons dance on your kitchen table. It's like Pokémon Go, but instead of catching cute monsters, you're being chased by them. Progress!

But the tech invasion of Halloween doesn't stop there. Oh no, we're just getting started. Let's talk about smart home Halloween decorations. Gone are the days when you had to manually turn on your spooky porch light. Now you can control your entire haunted house setup with your smartphone.

Want your ghost to start wailing at exactly 7:13 PM? There's an app for that. Need your animatronic werewolf to howl every time someone walks up your driveway? Just connect it to your smart doorbell. Want your Jack-o'-lanterns to change color based on the current phase of the moon? Weird flex, but okay.

The result is Halloween displays that would make Walt Disney jealous. Entire neighborhoods are turned into synchronized spooktaculars, with lights, sounds, and animations all perfectly timed. It's impressive, sure, but it also means that if your Wi-Fi goes down on Halloween night, your house suddenly becomes the lamest on the block. "Sorry, kids, the ghost is buffering."

But why stop at decorations? Technology is also changing the way we do costumes. 3D printing has opened up a whole new world of possibilities for costume creation. Want to be a perfectly screen-accurate Stormtrooper? Just download the files and print away. Need a last-minute accessory for your steampunk cowboy costume? Print it out. The only limit is your imagination... and the size of your 3D printer bed.

And let's not forget about "smart" costumes. We're talking outfits with built-in LED displays, sound effects, and even animatronics. Imagine a Transformer costume that actually transforms, or a chameleon outfit that changes color to match its surroundings. It's like cosplay met the Internet of Things and had a very nerdy baby.

Of course, all this tech comes with its own set of problems. Nothing ruins the spooky atmosphere quite like having to stop and recharge your costume mid-trick-or-treat. And good luck explaining to your kid why their $500 Iron Man costume with built-in repulsors can't go out in the rain.

But perhaps the biggest technological change to Halloween is happening in the world of social media. Halloween has always been a social holiday, but platforms like Instagram, TikTok, and YouTube have turned it into a full-blown online event.

People spend months planning elaborate costumes and decorations, all for that perfect viral post. Halloween makeup tutorials rack up millions of views. Pumpkin carving has gone from a fun family activity to a competitive sport, with people sharing increasingly intricate designs online.

It's like Halloween has become a performative act, with the whole world as our audience. "If a tree falls in a forest and no one is around to hear it, does it make a sound?" has become "If you wear an amazing Halloween costume and don't post a picture of it, did you even celebrate Halloween?"

This online Halloween culture has led to some interesting trends. "Halloweek" has become a thing, with people posting costume reveals every day leading up to Halloween. Pop culture costumes spread like wildfire, with everyone rushing to be the first to dress as the latest meme or TV character. It's like a global costume party where everyone's invited, but also everyone's competing.

But it's not all just fun and games. The pressure to have a "Pinterest-perfect" Halloween can be intense. People spend hundreds or even thousands of dollars on costumes and decorations, all for a holiday that lasts one night. It's enough to make you wonder: are we celebrating Halloween, or are we just creating content?

As we look to the future, it's clear that technology will continue to shape how we celebrate Halloween. But what exactly will that future look like? Well, let me dust off my crystal ball (which is actually just a Magic 8 Ball with some glitter glued to it) and make some predictions.

First up: AI-generated costumes and decorations. Imagine telling an AI, "I want to be a scary version of my accountant," and having it spit out a complete costume design. Or asking it to generate a unique monster for your haunted house. It's like playing mad scientist, but instead of body parts, you're stitching together lines of code.

We might also see the rise of "smart" trick-or-treating. Picture an app that maps out the best candy routes in your neighborhood, or lets you track your kids' location as they trick-or-treat. It could even rate houses based on the quality of their candy. "Avoid 42 Maple Street - they're handing out raisins again this year."

Virtual trick-or-treating could become more common, especially in areas where traditional trick-or-treating is difficult or dangerous. Kids could go door to digital door in a virtual neighborhood, collecting digital candy that gets translated into real treats delivered to their home. It's like DoorDash met Second Life and decided to celebrate Halloween.

We might even see the emergence of "Halloweenverse" - a Halloween-themed metaverse where people can celebrate together virtually. Imagine attending a costume party with people from all over the world, or exploring a haunted house that defies the laws of physics. It's like "Ready Player One," but with more candy corn.

But as we embrace these technological advancements, it's worth asking: what are we losing? Does a VR haunted house give you the same adrenaline rush as a real one? Can a digital Jack-o'-lantern ever replace the smell of pumpkin guts and the satisfaction of carving your own? Is trick-or-treating via app really the same as running from house to house with your friends?

There's something to be said for the tactile, sensory experience of traditional Halloween celebrations. The crunch of leaves under your feet as you trick-or-treat. The feel of a pumpkin's slimy insides as you scoop them out. The taste of that first bite of candy after a long night of collecting. Can technology ever truly replicate these experiences?

As we navigate this brave new world of high-tech Halloween, perhaps the key is finding a balance. Using technology to enhance our celebrations, rather than replace them entirely. After all, at its core, Halloween is about community, creativity, and a little bit of magic. And those are things that no amount of technology can replace.

So as we look to the future of Halloween, let's embrace the innovations that enhance our celebrations while holding onto the traditions that make the holiday special. After all, there's room for both VR ghosts and bedsheet ghosts in our Halloween festivities. Just maybe don't try to throw a sheet over your VR headset. That's a recipe for disaster, and not the fun, spooky kind.

In the end, whether you're celebrating Halloween with the latest tech gadgets or sticking to traditional bobbing for apples (which, let's be honest, has always been a weird tradition - who thought "Let's stick our faces in water to grab fruit with our teeth" was a good idea?), the most important thing is the spirit of the holiday. And no, I don't mean the spirits that supposedly roam the earth on Halloween. I mean the spirit of fun, creativity, and community that Halloween represents.

So go forth and celebrate, whether you're using an AI to design your costume or just throwing a sheet over your head and calling it a day. Because at the end of the day, Halloween is what we make of it. And if what we make of it involves robots, VR, and smart pumpkins, well, that's just the world we live in now. Happy haunting, tech ghouls and goblins!

Chapter 10: The Final Scare

Well, folks, we've reached the end of our spooky journey through the weird and wonderful world of Halloween. We've covered everything from ancient Celtic rituals to AI-generated costumes, from feminist witches to environmental impact, and from moral panics to high-tech hauntings. It's been a wild ride, hasn't it? Like a haunted house roller coaster, but with more candy and fewer safety regulations.

So what have we learned from this deep dive into all things Halloween? Well, for starters, we've learned that humans have been celebrating some form of Halloween for thousands of years. It seems that no matter how advanced we become as a society, we still have a primal need to dress up in silly costumes and demand candy from strangers. It's comforting, really, to know that our ancestors were just as weird as we are.

We've also learned that Halloween is a holiday of contradictions. It's a night when we celebrate fear, but in a fun way. It's a time when we embrace the macabre, but with a side of Reese's Pieces. It's an occasion that's ostensibly for children, but that adults seem to get way too invested in. It's like New Year's Eve met Dia de los Muertos and had a baby, and that baby grew up to be really into cosplay and sugar.

But perhaps most importantly, we've learned that Halloween is a mirror that reflects our society back at us, warts (witch's warts, of course) and all. Our Halloween celebrations show us who we are, what we value, and what we fear. And sometimes, what we see in that mirror is scarier than any haunted house or horror movie.

We've seen how Halloween becomes a battleground for larger cultural issues. Debates about costumes become debates about cultural sensitivity and appropriation. Arguments about trick-or-treating safety become arguments about community trust and childhood independence. Controversies over Halloween celebrations in schools become proxy wars for larger battles about religion in public life.

In a way, Halloween serves as a pressure release valve for society, allowing us to explore taboo topics and challenge social norms under the guise of "it's just a holiday." We can dress up as our deepest fears or our secret desires. We can indulge our sweet tooth without guilt. We can decorate our homes with skeletons and ghosts, turning death into a kitschy decoration rather than a terrifying inevitability. It's like a collective therapy session, but with more fake blood and less talking about our feelings.

We've also seen how Halloween has evolved over time, adapting to changing social norms and technological advancements. From its roots as a harvest festival marking the boundary between summer and winter, life and death, Halloween has become a multi-billion dollar industry encompassing everything from costumes and candy to haunted attractions and horror movies.

And yet, despite all these changes, the core of Halloween remains the same. It's still about community, about coming together to celebrate the spooky and the sweet. Whether we're gathering around a bonfire to ward off evil spirits or gathering around a TV to watch "Hocus Pocus" for the 47th time, we're still connecting with each other through shared traditions and experiences.

But as we look to the future of Halloween, we're faced with some scary questions (and not the fun kind of scary, like a haunted house, but the existential dread kind of scary, like realizing you're out of coffee on a Monday morning). How do we balance tradition with innovation? How do we celebrate in a way that's inclusive and respectful of all cultures? How do we keep the holiday fun and magical in a world that often seems all too real and frightening?

And perhaps most pressingly, how do we celebrate Halloween in a way that doesn't, you know, destroy the planet? Because let's face it, all those plastic decorations, disposable costumes, and individually wrapped candies aren't exactly eco-friendly. It's like we're trying to scare the environment to death, and unfortunately, it's working a little too well.

First up, let's talk about embracing creativity over consumerism. Instead of buying a new costume every year, why not make your own? Or swap with friends? Or wear the same costume for multiple years but come up with increasingly elaborate backstories for why your character is still around? "Yes, I'm still a zombie. I've been in zombie grad school. Do you know how long it takes to get a PhD when you're undead?" It's about time we had some representation for the academically ambitious undead.

Next, let's focus on experiences over stuff. Instead of buying a ton of decorations that will just end up in a landfill, why not invest in creating memorable experiences? Host a spooky storytelling night. Organize a neighborhood scavenger hunt. Have a pumpkin carving contest where the loser has to eat an entire pumpkin pie in one sitting. Okay, maybe not that last one, unless you want to turn your Halloween party into a re-enactment of "The Exorcist."

Now, let's talk cultural sensitivity. Before you put on that costume, ask yourself: "Is this celebrating a culture, or caricaturing it?" If you're not sure, err on the side of caution. There are plenty of costume ideas out there that don't involve appropriating someone else's culture. Be a sexy accountant instead. The world needs more sexy accountants. Nothing says "Halloween" quite like a well-balanced ledger.

When it comes to technology, use it to enhance, not replace, traditional celebrations. VR haunted houses are cool, but they shouldn't completely replace real-world experiences. After all, no AI can replicate the joy of seeing your neighbor's confused face when you show up at their door dressed as a "post-modern interpretation of existential dread." That's the kind of human interaction you just can't simulate.

Why not make Halloween a force for good? Organize a canned food drive along with trick-or-treating. Volunteer at a local shelter or food bank. Use your Halloween party as a fundraiser for a good cause. It's like trick-or-treating for your soul. Plus, it's a great way to offset the karmic debt you've incurred from all those years of toilet-papering your neighbor's trees.

Finally, keep the spirit of Halloween alive year-round. Who says you can only be creative, silly, and community-minded one night a year? Take the best parts of Halloween - the creativity, the sense of fun, the community spirit - and apply them to your everyday life. Just maybe leave the fake blood and spooky sound effects at home. Your coworkers will thank you, and you'll probably have an easier time getting through airport security.

So there you have it, folks. The future of Halloween: less stuff, more creativity, better costumes, and maybe, just maybe, a little bit more social consciousness. Who knows? Maybe by next Halloween, we'll have figured out how to use our powers of spookiness for good. And if not, well, there's always next year.

As we wrap up this spooktacular journey through the past, present, and future of Halloween, I hope you've gained a new appreciation for this weird and wonderful holiday. Whether you're a Halloween enthusiast who starts planning next year's costume on November 1st, or someone who views the holiday with a mixture of confusion and mild terror (and not the good kind of terror), there's no denying that Halloween has left an indelible mark on our culture.

So the next time you're carving a pumpkin, or putting on a costume, or sneaking another piece of candy from your kid's trick-or-treat haul (we all do it, no judgment here), take a moment to appreciate the rich history and complex cultural significance behind these seemingly silly traditions. And maybe, just maybe, let yourself get swept up in the magic of it all.

Because in the end, that's what Halloween is all about. It's about letting go of our everyday worries and embracing the fantastical, even if just for one night. It's about connecting with our communities, our histories, and our imaginations. It's about finding joy in the spooky, delight in the macabre, and sweetness in the scary.

So go forth, my fellow Halloween enthusiasts, and celebrate in whatever way feels right to you. Dress up as your favorite character, or your worst fear, or a pun so bad it makes people groan (I'm looking at you, "Cereal Killer" costume). Decorate your house like a gothic mansion, or a alien spaceship, or just stick a pumpkin on your porch and call it a day. Hand out full-sized candy bars and become a neighborhood legend, or turn off all your lights and pretend you're not home. It's your Halloween, and you can celebrate it however you want.

Just remember, as you're enjoying your candy corn and fake cobwebs, that you're part of a tradition that stretches back thousands of years. You're connecting with countless generations who have celebrated the changing of seasons, the thinning of veils between worlds, and the simple joy of dressing up and pretending to be someone (or something) else for a night.

And who knows? Maybe, just maybe, as you're out trick-or-treating or attending a costume party or watching a scary movie marathon, you'll feel a chill run down your spine. Maybe you'll catch a glimpse of something out of the corner of your eye that wasn't there a moment ago. Maybe you'll hear a whisper on the wind that sounds almost like words.

Because here's the thing about Halloween: for all our rational explanations and scientific understanding, there's still a part of us that wants to believe in magic. That wants to think that maybe, just maybe, on this one night of the year, the impossible becomes possible. That the spirits really do walk among us, that wishes made on jack-o'-lanterns really do come true, that there really is something special and magical about October 31st.

And you know what? Maybe there is. Maybe the real magic of Halloween isn't in ghosts or goblins or things that go bump in the night. Maybe it's in the way it brings us together, in the way it lets us explore our fears and fantasies, in the way it connects us to our past and our communities.

Or maybe I've just had too much candy corn and I'm getting sentimental. It's hard to tell at this point.

Either way, as we close the book on this exploration of all things Halloween, I hope you'll go out and make some spooky memories of your own. Eat too much candy. Stay up too late watching horror movies. Wear that ridiculous costume you've been too embarrassed to try. Embrace the weird, the wacky, and the wonderfully macabre spirit of Halloween.

Because life is short, and sometimes it's scary, but that doesn't mean we can't have fun with it. So put on your witch hat, light your jack-o'-lantern, and let's celebrate the most boo-tiful time of the year. Happy Halloween, everyone!

Thank you so much for reading my book about Halloween and remember, if you hear a strange noise in the middle of the night, if your jack-o'-lantern seems to be grinning a little too widely, if you coulda sworn that skeleton decoration just winked at you... well, it's probably nothing.

Probably.

Appendices

Appendix A: Spooky Stats and Fun Facts

Welcome to the part of the book where we throw a bunch of numbers and trivia at you faster than a hyperactive kid goes through their Halloween candy stash. Buckle up, buttercup, because things are about to get statistically spooky!

Did you know that Americans spend approximately $10 billion on Halloween each year? That's right, billion with a B. To put that in perspective, that's enough money to buy every person in Iceland a lifetime supply of candy corn. Not that anyone would want that much candy corn, but you get the point.

Speaking of candy, the average American consumes about 3.4 pounds of candy around Halloween. That's roughly the weight of a small pumpkin, or one very chonky cat. The most popular Halloween candy? Reese's Peanut Butter Cups. Apparently, nothing says "spooky season" quite like the combination of chocolate and peanut butter.

But it's not just candy that we're spending our hard-earned cash on. The average American spends about $86.27 on Halloween costumes, decorations, and candy. That's a lot of plastic vampire teeth and fake cobwebs, folks.

And speaking of costumes, did you know that adults are more likely to dress up for Halloween than kids? That's right, 67% of adults plan to celebrate Halloween, compared to only 62% of children. Who says growing up means you have to stop playing dress-up?

Here's a fun fact for you: the largest pumpkin pie ever made weighed 3,699 pounds and was over 20 feet in diameter. It was made in New Bremen, Ohio in 2010. That's one way to ensure everyone gets seconds at Thanksgiving, I suppose.

But let's not forget the spooky side of Halloween. According to a survey, 68% of Americans believe in ghosts. That's more than two-thirds of the population! I'm not saying it's because of all those "Ghost Hunters" marathons on TV, but I'm not not saying that either.

And here's a statistic that might actually scare you: Halloween is consistently one of the top three days for pedestrian injuries and fatalities. So maybe reconsider that all-black ninja costume, or at least add some reflective tape.

On a lighter note, the world record for fastest pumpkin carving is 16.47 seconds. The carving included eyes, nose, mouth, and ears. I'm not sure if it was a good carving, but it was certainly a fast one.

And finally, my personal favorite Halloween stat: 20% of pet owners dress up their pets for Halloween. That's one in five furry friends being subjected to the indignity of a hot dog costume or a doggy Dracula cape. But let's be honest, they look adorable and we all know it.

So there you have it, folks. A smorgasbord of Halloween stats and facts to impress your friends at your next costume party. Or to bore them to tears. Either way, you'll be the life of the party! Or the death of it. It is Halloween, after all.

Appendix B: Halloween Around the World

Alright, globe-trotters and armchair travelers, buckle up for a whirlwind tour of Halloween celebrations around the world. Because believe it or not, not everyone celebrates Halloween by dressing up as a sexy version of a household appliance and demanding candy from strangers. Shocking, I know.

Let's start with Mexico and their Día de los Muertos, or Day of the Dead. This celebration, which runs from October 31 to November 2, is like Halloween's more sophisticated, artsy cousin. Instead of running away from death, they embrace it, creating beautiful altars to honor deceased loved ones and having picnics in cemeteries. It's like a family reunion, but with more skulls and less awkward small talk.

In Ireland, the birthplace of Halloween, they celebrate pretty much like we do in the States, but with more bonfires and less lawsuit-inducing lawn decorations. They also play games like "snap-apple," where players try to bite an apple suspended on a string. It's like bobbing for apples, but with a higher risk of dental injury.

Over in China, they celebrate the "Hungry Ghost Festival" in the seventh month of the lunar calendar. They believe that during this time, the gates of hell open and ghosts are free to roam the earth. To appease these spirits, people offer food, money, and other goodies. It's like trick-or-treating, but in reverse, and with actual ghosts. Maybe.

In Germany, they hide their knives on Halloween night. This isn't to prevent any "Halloween" movie-style shenanigans, but to avoid harming the returning spirits. Apparently, German ghosts are very clumsy and prone to accidental stabbing.

The Philippines has a tradition called Pangangaluluwa, where children go door to door singing songs in exchange for prayers for the dead. It's like caroling, but spooky, and with more dead people.

In Japan, they celebrate the Obon Festival in August, where they honor the spirits of their ancestors. They hang lanterns everywhere to guide the spirits and perform dances. It's like a rave for ghosts, but with better lighting and less EDM.

And let's not forget about our friends down under in Australia. Halloween is still a relatively new concept there, and many Aussies resist it as an unwanted American cultural import. But those who do celebrate often have to get creative with their jack-o'-lanterns, sometimes using watermelons instead of pumpkins. Nothing says "spooky" quite like a carved watermelon, right?

So there you have it, a quick trip around the world of Halloween and Halloween-adjacent celebrations. Remember, no matter where you are in the world, there's probably a holiday that involves honoring the dead, dressing up in weird outfits, or eating way too much sugar. Humans are funny like that.

Appendix C: DIY Halloween Hacks

Alright, crafty witches and budget-conscious ghouls, gather 'round for some DIY Halloween hacks that'll make your celebration spookier than a ghost with student loan debt.

1. Toilet Paper Roll Eyes: Save those empty toilet paper rolls (I know you've got plenty after that Taco Bell incident). Cut eye shapes in them, stick a glow stick inside, and voila! You've got creepy eyes to hide in bushes. It's like your yard is judging everyone who walks by.

2. Trash Bag Spiderwebs: Take a black trash bag, cut it into a circle, then cut a spiral from the edge to the center. Stretch it out, and you've got a spiderweb that's probably sturdier than your first apartment.

3. Milk Jug Ghosts: Clean out some empty milk jugs (no, leaving them in the sun for a week doesn't count as cleaning), cut eyes in them, and stick a string of lights inside. Instant ghost army. Just don't blame me when they come to life and demand calcium.

4. Zombie Barbie: Take an old Barbie doll, mess up her hair, paint her face green, and rip up her clothes. Congratulations, you've just created Zombie Barbie, the toy that will definitely not give your children nightmares.

5. Banana Ghosts: Peel a banana halfway, use chocolate chips for eyes, and you've got a healthy Halloween snack that kids will definitely not throw in the trash in favor of candy.

6. Glowing Eyes in the Bushes: Cut eye shapes in a toilet paper roll, put a glow stick inside, and hide in bushes. Guaranteed to freak out at least one drunk party-goer.

7. Bleeding Candles: Drip red wax or paint down the sides of white candles for a creepy bloody effect. Perfect for that

"serial killer chic" look you've been going for.

8. Spooky Silhouettes: Cut spooky shapes out of black construction paper and tape them to your windows. From the outside, it'll look like your house is haunted. From the inside, it'll look like you've got a weird paper fetish.

9. Witch's Broom Parking: Stick a broom in the ground with a "Witch Parking Only" sign. It's cute, it's festive, and it might actually deter some of your neighbors from parking in front of your house.

10. Floating Candles: Hang battery-operated tea lights from your ceiling with fishing line for a Hogwarts Great Hall vibe. Just don't blame me when your acceptance letter from Hogwarts still doesn't come.

Remember, the best Halloween decorations are the ones that make your neighbors question your sanity while simultaneously being jealous of your creativity. Happy crafting!

Appendix D: Recommended Halloween Media

Alright, pop culture fiends and horror aficionados, it's time for a whirlwind tour through the graveyard of Halloween-related media. Grab your popcorn (or candy corn, if you're a monster), dim the lights, and let's dive in!

Movies:

1. "Halloween" (1978): Because nothing says "Happy Halloween" quite like a masked killer with mommy issues.
2. "Hocus Pocus" (1993): The movie that made an entire generation fall in love with Bette Midler as a buck-toothed witch.
3. "The Nightmare Before Christmas" (1993): Is it a Halloween movie or a Christmas movie? The correct answer is yes.
4. "Ghostbusters" (1984): Who you gonna call? Probably not the Ghostbusters, because they're fictional and you have real problems.
5. "Beetlejuice" (1988): The movie that taught us all that the afterlife is just as bureaucratic as real life, but with better interior design.
6. "It's the Great Pumpkin, Charlie Brown" (1966): Because nothing captures the spirit of Halloween quite like crushing disappointment and rocks in your trick-or-treat bag.
7. "The Rocky Horror Picture Show" (1975): It's not specifically a Halloween movie, but it's weird enough that it fits right in.
8. "Scream" (1996): The movie that taught us all the rules of horror movies, which we then promptly forgot in every subsequent horror movie.
9. "Practical Magic" (1998): For when you want your Halloween with a side of sisterhood and questionable

accents.

10. "Coraline" (2009): Because apparently, someone decided kids weren't having enough nightmares.

Books:

1. "Something Wicked This Way Comes" by Ray Bradbury: A carnival comes to town, bringing with it more than just cotton candy and rigged games.
2. "The Halloween Tree" by Ray Bradbury: Yes, another Bradbury. The man knew his spooky stuff.
3. "Dracula" by Bram Stoker: The OG vampire story, before vampires started sparkling and keeping diaries.
4. "The Legend of Sleepy Hollow" by Washington Irving: A classic tale of a headless horseman, or as I like to call it, "The Worst Uber Ride Ever."
5. "Scary Stories to Tell in the Dark" by Alvin Schwartz: The book that traumatized an entire generation of children, and we thank it for that.
6. "The Graveyard Book" by Neil Gaiman: Because being raised by ghosts is still probably easier than being a teenager.
7. "The Halloween Encyclopedia" by Lisa Morton: For when you want to be the most annoying person at the Halloween party with your "Did you know..." facts.
8. "Halloweenland" by Al Sarrantonio: A town where it's always Halloween? Sign me up! (But also, where do they get their non-Halloween supplies? These are the questions that keep me up at night.)
9. "Dark Harvest" by Norman Partridge: A small town, a pumpkin-headed monster, and a bunch of teenage boys with guns. What could possibly go wrong?
10. "The Night Country" by Stewart O'Nan: A ghost story that's more melancholy than scary, for when you want your

Halloween with a side of existential crisis.

TV Shows:

1. "The Simpsons Treehouse of Horror" specials: Because nothing says "Halloween" quite like yellow cartoon characters parodying classic horror stories.
2. "Stranger Things": Not specifically a Halloween show, but it's got enough 80s nostalgia and creepy monsters to fit right in.
3. "American Horror Story": Each season is a new flavor of nightmare fuel.
4. "The Addams Family": The original goth family, before being goth was cool.
5. "Buffy the Vampire Slayer": Teen drama meets monster hunting. What's not to love?
6. "Over the Garden Wall": A miniseries that captures the eerie, melancholy feeling of autumn perfectly.
7. "The Twilight Zone": Classic sci-fi and horror that still holds up today. Just don't binge-watch it unless you want to question your entire reality.
8. "Gravity Falls": A kids' show that's somehow both adorable and deeply unsettling.
9. "What We Do in the Shadows": Vampire roommates trying to navigate modern life. It's like "Friends," but with more blood-sucking.
10. "Supernatural": Fifteen seasons of monster hunting, brotherly angst, and inexplicably attractive demons.

Podcasts:

1. "Lore": For when you want your Halloween with a side of historical accuracy.
2. "Welcome to Night Vale": A surreal, hilarious, and sometimes

terrifying look at a town where every conspiracy theory is true.

3. "The NoSleep Podcast": Because who needs sleep anyway?
4. "Scared to Death": Real people share their scariest experiences. Listen with the lights on.
5. "Haunted Places": Explore the history and hauntings of real locations around the world.

Remember, consuming any or all of this media does not actually make you an expert in ghost hunting, vampire slaying, or witch crafting. Please leave the supernatural battles to the fictional professionals.

And there you have it, folks! A comprehensive guide to Halloween media that should keep you entertained (and possibly sleepless) until next Halloween. Use this knowledge wisely, and remember: the scariest monster of all is the one that eats all your Halloween candy when you're not looking. Happy haunting!

About the Author

I grew up in a small town, where my love for books blossomed at an early age. With a bookshelf brimming with fantasy adventures and witty memoirs, I spent countless hours lost in the pages of authors who could weave words into magic. This enthusiasm for reading naturally evolved into a fascination with writing.After graduating college, I began my career in marketing as a ghostwriter, specializing in blog posts and articles for various clients. This role allowed me to flex my creative muscles and experiment with different voices and styles while honing my craft. However, despite enjoying this work, the dream of publishing my own books lingered in the background.While I found joy in writing for others, a persistent anxiety loomed over the thought of sharing my personal thoughts, stories and ideas with the world. The fear of judgment and failure led to years of hesitation. But after many late-night brainstorming sessions, I had a life-changing realization: every author starts somewhere, and embracing vulnerability is part of the journey.With renewed determination and a desire to connect with readers, I decided to step into the spotlight under the fictive pen name A.D. Wryte. This decision symbolizes my commitment to authenticity and my promise to write not just for the sake of publication, but to share books that inspire, entertain, and resonate with others.